To my dear friend Teresa,
may God continue to
bless the journey you
are on & may our friendship
reignite!

WHY

curse the

darkness

WHEN YOU CAN LIGHT A CANDLE?

♡ Patti Garibay
2020
Psalms 78:6-7

WHY
curse the
darkness
WHEN YOU CAN LIGHT A CANDLE?

PATTI GARIBAY

Carpenter's Son Publishing

Published by Carpenter's Son Publishing, Franklin, Tennessee

Published in association with Larry Carpenter of
Christian Book Services, LLC
www.christianbookservices.com

Edited by Danise DiStasi and Anita Agers-Brooks

Cover Design by Suzanne Lawing and Becky Lipps

Interior Layout Design by Suzanne Lawing

Cover photo by Lauren Burrows

Printed in the United States of America

978-1-949572-86-5

DEDICATIONS

- To the Lord God whose love and belief in me allowed a candle to be lit and continued to provide the fuel for the past twenty-five years. His calling to write this book was made clear to me when I read Psalms 78:6 which says, *"So the next generation would know them, even the children yet to be born and they in turn would tell their children. Then they would put their trust in God and would not forget his deeds, but would keep his commands."*

- To my parents whose love, support, guidance, and example made me the woman I am today.

- To Pat, my beloved, who helped to write our life story and this book. His support through this process has been tremendous and he once more has made my dreams come true.

- To my children, Rachael, Meghan, Katy, and Jon, along with my sons and daughters-in-love, and my grandbabies—you are the joy of my life.

- To all of those who came alongside during the AHG journey and continue to serve in this vital ministry, may the Lord bless you for all of your days.

SPECIAL ACKNOWLEDGEMENTS

- Danise DiStasi, whose gifts and talents launched this project.

- Anita Agers-Brooks, whose writing proficiency polished the manuscript.

- Rachael Culpepper, my little lamb, whose strength, intelligence, and encouragement made this book possible.

- Kathleen Fitzsimmons, whose talent, tenacity, joy, love, and patience buoyed me throughout this adventure.

CONTENTS

PREFACE

"When are you going to write your book?" so many have asked over the years.

"Someday," was my typical response.

Honestly, I never really thought I would. I recall Ernest Hemingway's advice to writers. "Write hard and clear about what hurts." I feared unpeeling my emotional onion and exposing myself to the pain and heartache I'd spent much of my life working to overcome. Yet, I sensed a very strong calling from the Lord that this book needed to be written, despite my feelings surrounding it.

I pray by sharing my story, other men and women might feel encouraged to look at their own pilgrimage, and the many ways God artfully ordered their steps. There's always a greater plan than what we can see in the moment we are walking through dark adversity. That's why we need Him to light our way.

I've been accused of wearing rose-colored glasses on more than one occasion. I do prefer to see the positive in situations, perhaps that is why I never look back. I keep moving forward. My eyes-on-the-horizon view may also serve as a way to help me move past the mistakes I have made.

God's plan for our lives is also similar to the creation of a tapestry. In Colossians 2:2, Paul says, "I want you woven into a tapestry of love, in touch with everything there is to know of God."

The tapestry of love God has woven for each of us is unique, and each an incredible work from a creative Maker. As humans, we often see only the back side of our tapestry—a jumbled mess of threads and knots that make no sense whatsoever. Yet, in God's perfect timing, He allows us to see the beautiful work of art that is our life, and the reasons for certain threads to color its fabric.

Throughout the weaving process of my life, even amidst the darkest knots, there has been one golden thread: God's faithfulness and patience. As my husband, Pat, and I have learned obedience and submission, we've experienced many blessings. However, this book is not about what Pat or I have done. The accumulation of our actions led to the peace found only in a life surrendered in trust to the Lord.

To use another metaphor, you truly cannot walk on water unless you get out of the boat. And who doesn't want to walk above their problems? Fixing our eyes on our Savior will bring us to places of which we can only dream. And a relationship with Him will grow us in spaces we never knew we could experience, those that often begin in dark places.

So, whether we need a spiritual candle to shed light on the beauty that exists on the backside of our tangles, or one that enables us to see beyond the wind and waves of current circumstances, I want you to know it's available. I hope by sharing parts of my life story and lessons learned along the way, you are inspired and encouraged to take the next step in following Jesus.

Our God does not need us to accomplish His purposes. He will accomplish what He wills, whether we obey or not. But when we join in His call, we discover blessings beyond measure and fulfillment unimaginable. The road to the founding of the American Heritage Girls has been an adventure, a quest, and a service, fitting of our one true King.

In the coming pages, I will share the heartache, joy, pain, and victories that truly brought beauty out of ashes. God is so faithful, and He wants to do this for you, too. Invite Him into your concerns and fears and watch Him light up your world in ways that will astound you and those who watch your transformation. A candle is most visible and appreciated when it beats back the darkness. I know, because God lit one in me.

CHAPTER ONE

RELEASED

March 8, 2004

I had imagined this day and dreaded its arrival. The pungent smell of incense mixed with floral bouquets wafted through the air of the old church. Memories flooded my mind, and they reinforced the knowledge that no amount of preparation could have strengthened me for facing the reality of our good-byes.

I tenderly brushed the edge of the American flag draped on his casket, its stars and stripes a testament to all the years he spent serving others so well. He'd endured such pain and suffering, and yet his sweet spirit shined through to the end.

I touched the smooth, gray fabric of his jacket. A tear rolled down my face. "Finally, at rest now, Dad," I said. "You've made such a difference in my life and in many others."

I'd spent years not trusting God because of my misconception that He was the author of suffering in this world. For the majority of my life, Dad's incurable illness created a mental roadblock for my soul, preventing me from seeking the love of God.

Dad lay so peacefully, probably the most peaceful I'd seen him in years. I thought to myself, *Oh how I will miss you. You were such a tower of strength, despite your inability to stand. You were a gentle shepherd to our family, and I know you desperately wanted to carry us despite your frailty.* His four decades of enduring an acute, chronic illness had finally ended.

I opened the clasp of a small American Heritage Girls pin and attached it to his lapel, then straightened it, smoothed his jacket, and smiled. With that, I leaned over and whispered, "Thank you for encouraging me. I love you. I'll miss you, and I will continue the good fight." I kissed his bald head—I'd said good-bye for the very last time.

My husband, Pat, always the supportive, loving man, stood next to me with my children on the other side. The sun shone into the narthex (what some might call a foyer) of the church through stained-glass windows, radiating a bright glow on my father's casket. It was a suitable farewell. As the song, "I Can Only Imagine," by Mercy Me played, I watched the dust particles dance in a sunbeam. I envisioned my dad the minute he stepped into heaven, no longer bound by his wheelchair or crippled by his horrible disease. He stood healthy and strong. I will hold that picture dearly in my heart, until the day he and I are reunited in Heaven.

The service culminated with a twenty-one gun salute at Spring Grove Cemetery. With each resounding discharge, my soul grieved, leaving teardrop shaped stains on my blouse.

After final prayers, our celebration of Dad's life ended when his casket was lowered into his final place of rest. We played Roger Miller, his favorite musician, from a boom box we had brought from home. My oldest sister Mary Sue, an amazing artist, had designed a beautiful, family monument years before—we would add Dad's name plate later, when it was delivered.

A father leaves a lasting mark on a person's life—positive or negative, good or bad—but the ultimate result depends on what we do in response. My dad was the first man I ever loved. He was also instrumental in setting me on the path I now walk. Little did he know the influence he made in my life would ultimately affect tens of thousands of girls in the future.

> I have learned it is always best to talk to your hurting friends. Even if you don't think your words will bring comfort, people will know you care.

As with any ending, my dad's death forced me to make a choice about the next direction I would take. For forty-five years I was the third daughter to my father, Norm. He was a priority to me, as many of my life choices hinged on his well-being. Celebrations, life events, and holidays were all adapted to include him. Now what would I do? Would I stay stuck in grief, mourning my loss, or would I use my father's inspiration to make an impact for the future? The decision was mine to make. I understood that clearly, but it did not make my next steps any easier.

HAVE YOU CONSIDERED . . .

- *Why would a "good" God allow suffering?*
- *Have you ever known anyone who was physically or mentally disabled, yet provided great inspiration?*

- *How have you been impacted by a strong warrior, perhaps someone who fought the good fight and taught you lessons to their final breath? What part of their example do you want to follow? Read 2 Timothy 4:7 that says, "I have fought the good fight, I have finished the race, I have kept the faith."*

- *How can we as a society honor the contributions of those with disabilities?*

- *If you have lost a parent, have you had a shift in your understanding of who you are?*

CHAPTER TWO

CAMELOT

1931–1959

I was the third daughter born to Norm and Jean Haverkos. The love story of my parents was not always one for storybooks, though the way it began had a fairytale feel.

Dad was born on March 17, 1931, and was raised on a family farm in Oldenburg, Indiana. Hard work was a normal routine; whether he fed chickens and gathered their eggs, tried to avoid cow kicks as he milked, or removed manure with a pitchfork, Dad rarely stopped from early morning until late at night. While he toiled, he dreamed of playing professional baseball, and spent what little leisure time he had pitching and fielding in the rocky barnyard.

Short, stocky, and nicknamed "Toughie," Dad threw the fastest ball in the county. Norm Haverkos was a power player at Batesville High School. The son of second-generation German immigrant parents, Dad's means were limited, so his baseball scholarship was welcomed. Dad attended Ball State University, for his undergrad degree in mathematics and then Purdue University, where he earned a degree in electrical engineering. Dad's scholarship reminds me of the providential hand of God on our family—his marriage to my mother provides even more evidence of that fact.

My mom, Emma Jean Wallpe, was born in 1934. Her parents were also farmers in St. Maurice, Indiana.

"Jeanie," as she was affectionately called, attended a one-room schoolhouse, yet earned a scholarship from a private Catholic School in the nearby community of Oldenburg, Indiana. She was one of the rare commuters who traveled to and from school, while most students resided in the dormitories of the Immaculate Conception Academy. During high school, she and her family moved to Batesville. She excelled at her studies, was the secretary of her class, and worked part-time jobs at the five-and-dime and town jewelers. Jeanie was a pretty brunette whose bubbly, "Hi," helped her strike up conversations with friends and strangers she met on the street.

My parents fell in love during high school, after meeting at a barn dance in Batesville, Indiana. In those days, for fifteen cents, you could enjoy a night of music and dance and potentially find a spouse. What a deal!

Norm and Jean married in 1953, and my sister, Mary Sue, was born in 1954. A few months later, Dad was served with a military notice. The draft gave him no choice but to enlist in the Army.

My parents were just figuring out how to live as a family when Dad suddenly had to prepare for service in Okinawa. This was devastating news for my mom.

> I can clearly see what perhaps my mom never saw— God was using this life-altering situation to prepare her for the storms to come.

She didn't even know how to drive. How would she handle parenting alone?

Mom sat on the bed in their little apartment and wept, sad and lonely, night after night, scared to take the next step. As I reflect back, I can clearly see what perhaps my mom never saw—God was using this life-altering situation to prepare her for the storms to come. My mom would find herself on the edge of a bed asking "What am I going to do next?" many times.

This was not the picture she had envisioned of married life. However, Mom's focus, intelligence, and work ethic helped her survive. As was common at the time, my mom and her new baby moved back to Batesville to live with her mother and father while Dad served overseas.

Two years later, when Dad returned after spending 1954 through 1956 as an Army radar repairman and repair instructor, he finished his engineering degree at Purdue University. No more than a year later, my sister, Karen, was born.

In 1959, my parents moved to Norwood, Ohio, where I entered the world on March 27, a somber Good Friday complete with rain and dense fog. And even though I was not the longed-for son, according to my sisters I immediately captured the heart of my daddy. My brother, Tim, arrived in 1962 and took care of a male namesake, completing our family unit.

Dad's job transferred us to the Boston, Massachusetts area, where he worked in the Applied Technology Division at AVCO. He and a team of engineers were assigned to perfect the thermal protection system for the Apollo command module. After traveling through extreme temperatures in outer space, this thermal protection system shielded astronauts against the surface heat that rose to approximately 5000°F during their re-entry to the earth's atmosphere. My dad's teeny-tiny role in the crazy 1960s dream of people landing on the moon still fills me with pride today.

During that era, my parents were fans of the newly elected president, John F. Kennedy, and were excited about moving to his state. They loved the sense of connectedness they felt to him as a Catholic with a young family, just like them. They had no idea President Kennedy's term would be short-lived, due to his tragic death.

When he was assassinated, my mom bought a copy of *Life* magazine with a cover that featured the mourning family of John F. Kennedy: Jackie, Caroline, and John-John. Mom read an article to us, where Jackie referenced a line from the Lerner and Loewe musical, *Camelot*, to describe the Kennedy era White House. "Don't let it be forgot, that once there was a spot, for one brief shining moment, that was known as Camelot." Jackie indicated that it was one of Kennedy's favorite lyrics from the musical and added, "There'll be great presidents again, but there'll never be another Camelot again. It will never be that way again."[1]

Following the untimely death of JFK, Mom and Dad bought the *Camelot* soundtrack on 33 rpm vinyl. As a eulogy to our fallen president and the hope my parents shared for the future of the country and perhaps their marriage, they played it regularly. I think in their own way, Mom and Dad were hoping to create their own form of Camelot—a hopeful idealism that featured chivalry and the legendary King Arthur and his Queen Guinevere.

---

1 Source cited: *Life Magazine*, December 6, 1963, pg. 49 interview with Theodore H. White

In spite of our nation's dark moment, I enjoyed life in Massachusetts during the Sixties. Even at four years old, I played a tour guide of sorts. When visitors came, a regular occurrence, we followed a general site-seeing itinerary, including the Bunker Hill Monument. I led the way determinedly, curls bouncing, as I climbed all 294 steps. Despite my young age and short legs, I always reached the top first. Though I was the third daughter and an unlikely captain, my role as leader of something was clearly established, even then.

Everything seemed normal. We enjoyed family trips to the beach where we found lobsters and held birthday celebrations by taking day trips to Boston on the exciting subway. My sisters and I spent hours in our bedrooms twirling to the sounds of Tchaikovsky's *The Nutcracker Suite* in our crisp crinoline slips. Each day, I eagerly awaited my dad's nightly return from work, hopeful and secure. But, soon, Mom noticed that Dad was experiencing some difficulties. Though I was young, I knew something was wrong, and the news we were about to receive would alter our lives forever. Some of us lose our innocence far earlier than we're prepared for.

HAVE YOU CONSIDERED . . .

- *Have you spent a lot of time dreaming about what your perfect future might be?*

- *Have you envisioned your own version of Camelot?*

- *How do you handle disappointment when your ideal picture becomes interrupted by life-altering news?*

- *Are you open to rejecting your own Camelot, in order to embrace the better plan Christ has perfectly created for you?*

CHAPTER THREE

DIAGNOSIS

1963–1966

He would get up to walk—and stumble—over nothing. Dad was always active and very fit, so the physical changes he experienced were noticeable. He had trouble doing everyday chores and became very frustrated, which was not his normal behavior. Even his beloved hobbies were affected. I loved to watch him play recreational baseball, but he suddenly complained about double vision and had trouble seeing the ball, much less catching it.

Now, he often sat in his big, comfortable chair and rubbed his legs. I overheard him tell my mom that it felt like rubber bands were wound around his knees, and he felt as if his circulation was being cut off. I never knew him to go to the doctor before, so when he sought medical help, I knew my dad had to be sick.

His doctors ran a battery of tests over several long weeks. We waited and we waited for the results. Dad seemed to get worse with each passing day until finally, the diagnosis came back. Dad had multiple sclerosis (MS).

My world began spinning. In 1963, very little was known about MS, which made the disease even more frightening. Nothing felt secure and nothing felt safe. Camelot was falling.

My mom said she felt the same way when she learned Dad was drafted to Okinawa—totally ill-equipped to deal with the reality that her life would not play out as she had imagined. Upon hearing Dad's diagnosis, Mom once more sat on the edge of the bed, feeling hopeless and alone.

My parents traveled to a Boston-area hospital to learn what they could about the disease. After gaining a basic understanding of what they were facing, my mother traveled back to Indiana where she shared the news with my paternal grandparents. They didn't fully understand MS or how it would impact our family—no one did. Was it terminal? Was it contagious? Could it have been caused by his radar work in Okinawa? Could there possibly be a cure?

Because of what so many people in their generation had experienced with polio, people were fearful of any disease. At that time, the big news in the medical world was the development and success of organ transplants. You didn't hear health experts talking about saving the lives of people with MS.

Amid the chaos of navigating this new diagnosis, Dad's Apollo command module project in Boston was completed. We moved back to Cincinnati, into a new house in a new neighborhood. There were many things I loved about our new home, but the fruit trees in the backyard were among my favorites.

The summer after our move, the branches on one of the trees bowed with plump, juicy peaches. Dad created props to hold the peach tree branches up so they wouldn't break, and the fruit could continue to ripen. Dad was still able to walk, but each day it became more and more difficult for him.

One day, Dad went to the side yard to pick fruit from the tree. There were several peaches already on the ground, which made stepping very uneven. He struggled to keep his balance but slipped and fell, breaking his leg. For most people, his injuries would have required a cast and a pair of crutches, but this fall placed my dad in a wheelchair—a wheelchair he would need for the rest of his life.

This single incident changed everything in the dynamics of our family. Mom's unwavering resolve and her conviction to find relief and treatment filled her every thought. She worked to create simple adaptations for Dad, like a wheelchair ramp into our front door, and creating changes to his diet. Dad was determined, too.

My dad wanted to participate in clinical trials for MS patients, one of which used experimental drugs and required hospitalization. Even though he knew he might not personally benefit, my dad was still willing to be a "guinea pig," in hopes the research might help others in the future.

He was able to take some treatments from home—including a remedy called the "ice treatment." Some claimed the cooling affect allowed more neuro signals to move across the damaged nerves, supposedly allowing for pain relief and increased mobility. So, every other evening, we gently guided Dad to the ground in the kitchen, where he would lie on a plastic mat my mother had made.

We filled big, plastic milk jugs with water and froze them. We then cut the plastic off the frozen jugs, so only chunks of ice were left. Next, we soaked towels in a frigid ice bath and wrung them out, shaking our bare, numb, stinging hands between turns, to keep our blood flowing.

My job was to put the freezing towels on my dad's legs. I then had to lie on his legs to keep them from violently tremoring, in hopes of keeping the iced towels in place. Time and again, I gripped his cold, wet, towel-draped shins and fought the tremors from his legs, matched by those in my freezing fingers.

A few times, I peeked up from the task and looked at my father's face, his eyes closed, and his face wrinkled in agony. Ultimately, the scene was too painful for my empathic heart and I made a habit of no longer looking up. I dreaded those "ice-treatment" days and I am sure Dad did as well.

Thankfully, Dad's MS only challenged him physically. He remained cognitively sharp. Despite the lack of resources for living with MS in those days, my dad's natural ingenuity, work experience, and determination proved to be useful in the adaptation process. He installed hand controls on his car, so he was able to continue working. He was passionate about his job and fought hard to continue his career, even if that meant needing help from co-workers getting in and out of his vehicle.

As an electrical engineer, Dad worked with computers, which at the time were a new technology. His piercing blue eyes lit up like a child's when he described the size of the computers he got to work with daily. "Why, they are the size of an entire building!" he said, using hand motions to help describe the power and potential in this new phenomenon.

Despite all the challenges, my parents tried to remain socially active. Together, they started playing bridge in a couple's league but because of Dad's disability, my parents often felt like outsiders. This created even more stress, especially for my extroverted mom. Bitterness began to grow from her loneliness. She felt no one understood her plight, and the most devastating part for her was that most people didn't even try—or so it seemed.

As an adult, I've often considered that perhaps people cared, but the unique nature of my parents' situation made others feel uncomfortable. Many chose not to engage with Dad and Mom, likely due to their own fear of inadequacy instead of an aversion to my parents. Regardless of the real reasons, because of the loss of relationships my parents endured, I have learned it is always best to talk to your hurting friends. Even if you don't think your words will bring comfort, people will know you care. Silence and avoidance, perceived as rejection, hurt more than saying the wrong thing.

> I have learned it is always best to talk to your hurting friends. Even if you don't think your words will bring comfort, people will know you care.

Professional counseling was rarely sought in the Sixties, and my mother was no exception. Unable to let go of her dreams and the "what should have beens," Mom turned to Camelot-negativity and the numbing effects of alcohol as outlets for her pain and frustration. Life seemed unfair to my mother, and her anger, typically directed toward my dad, erupted often.

I went to bed many nights, listening to my mother rage at a man I knew as a very caring and loving soul. It was hard to watch our family unravel. There were times I couldn't listen to the yelling anymore. So, as the nightly background noise of screaming escalated outside my room, I tried to escape into my own little fantasy world. I read biographies of famous patriots from history or escaped to the adventures of Pippi

Longstocking and her exciting travels. But I never got to hide long enough.

The clinking of ice in the glass, as my mom poured another drink, often brought me abruptly back to the reality I wanted to get away from. For the little girl with the bouncing curls, it felt like someone came and took her Mommy and Daddy away. I felt like it should have been happening to someone else.

I knew my parents loved each other, but their love was not enough to deal with the giant called MS. They needed supernatural love, the kind of love God provides through the atonement of His Son and by living through the Holy Spirit.

As human beings, our love has limits, but God's love does not. I so wish my mom had known earlier about the power enacted when Jesus died on the cross and was resurrected from the grave. I wish her faith had grown during that difficult time. But sadly, I cannot say this was so. The loving mother the little girl with bouncing curls once knew was gone, and the painful period of my childhood had only just begun.

HAVE YOU CONSIDERED . . .

- *Has bitterness ever harbored in your soul when life suddenly became difficult?*
- *Have you ever felt hopeless, alone, and misunderstood during a painful period in your life?*
- *Why does human love fall short in times of turmoil?*

CHAPTER FOUR

IDENTITY

1967

I felt guilty asking for it, because I knew the amount of stress my mom dealt with every day. I finally drummed up enough nerve to make my request.

Even at eight years old, I was wired for relationship. I made friends easily and wanted a birthday sleepover, but instead, Mom agreed to an afternoon celebration. That was somewhat disappointing, since I longed to have an overnight party, but I'd learned to be grateful for what I could get.

I hand-drew and meticulously colored the invitations and gave them to five friends. On the big day, I held my breath, until one by one, my friends arrived. I was thrilled. We ate cake and ice cream and played a few games. It didn't matter who won, just playing made us giggle so hard we struggled to catch our breath. I was happy to be with my friends and to feel like a normal kid, even if it was only for a single afternoon.

As I romped and laughed, I caught a glimpse of my mom, who appeared exhausted and overwhelmed. It was in this moment, I purposed in my heart that this party would be my first and last request.

How could I expect my mom to take care of a disabled husband, raise four kids, and attempt to cater to my childish desires? I was certain my inferior needs would soon cause more resentment and anger to well up in my mother, making my father suffer as a result. It was my duty to forget this dream of future birthday celebrations. I vowed when I grew up, things would be different. I was determined that my children would have parties they would always remember fondly, including sleepovers with fancy cakes, tons of friends, and big, bright balloons.

Once my short-lived, party era of life passed, we still celebrated birthdays, just on a smaller scale. One year, Mom made a ceramic Charlie Brown figurine for me, and I loved that gift. I treasured the thought of my mother patiently painting each line of Charlie's shirt just for me. I put it in a place of honor on my bedroom shelf. Sometimes, I'd lay in my bed at night and stare at Charlie Brown, imagining a day of tea-time with my mom and shopping excursions that lasted the whole afternoon.

I do believe my mother tried the best she could. Despite her full-time job and daily stress from caring for Dad, Mom continued to make room for activities meant to support the well-being of her children. She brought us to our Girl Scout meetings, paid for us to have art lessons, allowed us to play sports, and drove us to Mass every Sunday, all while making sure we learned good values, knowing right from wrong.

Although I longed for Mom's time and attention, Dad always seemed to have plenty of both. Whenever I was at home, I followed my dad around just to be near him. My sister, Karen, teased a few times that I was "Dad's darling," because I looked so much like our mom. Because of my darling status, there were times my siblings had me ask Dad for special treats or favors.

I'll admit that I liked to please my older sisters, and I had an uncanny knack for getting my dad to do what we wanted. But ultimately, the extra time spent with him was what I was really after.

Dad seemed to enjoy time with me as well, no matter the place or season of year. Our family's garage was our "special" meeting place. In the winter months, we warmed the garage with a space heater while refinishing antiques or caning chairs. Dad's hobbies soon became my hobbies. However, in the summer of 1967, I had just finished third grade and I had an idea for a hobby of my own. As usual, Dad indulged.

I decided to have school in our special meeting place during summer break. Somehow, I convinced neighborhood kids to attend my pretend "institute" during those sweltering months in my non-air-conditioned garage. I became the teacher I always wanted to be, set up desks, and even served popsicles for snacks. I had everything I needed to run an efficient and effective classroom—date stampers, stickers, a chalk board (complete with a pointer), and even a bell. My schoolroom provided just the right amount of escape and purpose during the long summer break for the kids in the neighborhood, but even more for myself. Though some of my students knew about my dad, none of them knew of the difficulties "Miss Patti" faced after the bell rang at the end of our school day. I stayed in "professional character" while in the classroom.

My formative years were split, some time spent in a world of love and acceptance from my dad, and other times spent in a world of rejection and escape. My mom's rage was no longer aimed solely at my father. My siblings and I became recipients of her verbal lashings and criticism. It didn't take long for her words to penetrate my heart, allowing insecurities to rush in, filling its many vulnerable spaces.

In retrospect, I realize this foundation started me on a years-long struggle with my self-worth and identity. We all need validation that our lives are meaningful. And because affirmations are so important, any criticism is hurtful, especially from our parents. This deep world of rejection would haunt me into my adulthood.

> We all need validation that our lives are meaningful. And because affirmations are so important, any criticism is hurtful, especially from our parents.

Because of the yelling I frequently heard from my mom, while my disabled father shrunk in guilt, I was a very fear-filled child. I cowered at night, scared of the verbal assaults, finding only one single comfort, sucking my thumb. Insecurities seeped in and I believed lies to be true about myself: *You aren't worthy. You aren't smart. You cause additional strife*, and so on. Those mental messages took a lifetime to identify and intentional work to move beyond.

Relief didn't arrive until I learned about the true nature of God and comprehended what it meant to be His child. I had to understand more about Him to understand more about me. I needed to realize that "people approval" only lasts for a moment, but God's mercy and love are eternal. His embrace is so much more fulfilling than anything offered by a human heart. His acceptance is the only affirmation and validation that will wholly satisfy us—yet, we don't have to give up on being acceptable in the eyes of other people. God sometimes sends surprising gifts.

In my youth, I had yet to learn my value as a treasured child of God. And in third grade, little did I know that human validation was coming by way of a brunette boy from Pittsburgh. The Garibay family moved into the parish, and life once again changed.

HAVE YOU CONSIDERED . . .

- *Where do you seek affirmation and validation?*
- *Are you able to see the difference between self-care and selfishness?*
- *Where does your inner security come from?*

CHAPTER FIVE

THE BOY FROM THE "BURGH"

1967

We were excited to meet this family of seven, mostly because my older sisters thought Pat Garibay's brothers were very cute. Pat and his family moved into our area in 1967, after his father's transfer from Pittsburgh, Pennsylvania to Cincinnati. While Pat and I attended St. John's Elementary together and hung out with the same kids, we really did not get to know each other until years later.

Pat was born on Friday, February 13, 1959 (he used to blame his bad luck on his "unfortunate" day of birth, but I knew better) in Pittsburgh, Pennsylvania. He was the fourth child of Rob and Connie Garibay. Since the typical child is subconsciously influenced to a greater degree by their same sex parent, it's no surprise that the challenging life Pat's father experienced fed into the man my husband became.

Rob Garibay was raised in the Great Depression by a single mother who was a very strong woman in a difficult time. Due to hardships in her immediate family, she had taken on the role of matriarch for her siblings and disabled sister, becoming the stable center for those she loved.

When the Depression hit during her young adult years, Rob's father, a Mexican immigrant, felt it best to return to the wealth of his family in Mexico to insure a livelihood. This was a step "Grandma Airplane," as she became known to her grandkids, was not willing to make. She had an extended family she felt responsible for and couldn't see any way to leave them. Rob's father left the family in Chicago, never to be seen again.

The void left behind by his father's sudden departure was substantial, and its impact never left Rob. Pat's father worked hard to support the family, including riding his bicycle to work at a Chinese restaurant when he was eight or nine years old. Stories like these are prevalent in Garibay family lore. Rob also became a lifeguard in high school on the beaches of Chicago's Lake Michigan, he joined the Navy in 1942 at age seventeen, and he rose in the ranks to become a Golden Glove boxer. As part of the U.S. military's "Greatest Generation," Rob became a flight engineer on a World War II reconnaissance plane which flew over the Pacific Ocean where he was shot down. He was the kind of man from which legends are made.

Connie, Pat's mom, was born in 1925 and grew up in a small town called Nanty Glo, Pennsylvania. Her deep faith was the cornerstone of her life. She loved the Lord with all her heart and wanted nothing more than to serve Him and His people. Connie also had a deep sense of patriotism and relished the freedoms her country afforded her, so when the war effort began, she was ready to serve. She enlisted in the Army as a nurse, serving in Hawaii, with a final tour in occupied Japan.

Rob and Connie were set up by friends on a blind date, and after a quick courtship that lasted only six months, they married. They started their life in Chicago, eventually moving to Galena, Illinois, where Pat's two older brothers were born. Their next stop was Pittsburgh, which became the birthplace of Pat and his two sisters.

Connie experienced many losses in her life. Her older brother died at the age of twenty-two, she lost two babies, and she experienced the deaths of her grandmother and mother to cancer at fairly young ages. In her later years, the death of a seventeen-year-old granddaughter rocked my mother-in-law, and finally, she lost her own health to the same cancer that took her Grandma and mom. Relying on her faith gave Connie the strength to make it through many difficult times. She loved Pat's father, Rob, very much, but their marriage was not free from its share of problems.

> Pat wanted to act in opposition from the example he had seen and resolved that he would be a different type of husband and father.

Early in his life, Pat noticed there was an underlying level of disrespect in how his father treated his mother. A blanket of anger also seemed to influence Rob Garibay's engagement with his children. As a man, Pat wanted to act in opposition from the example he had seen and resolved that he would be a different type of husband and father.

Pat's heart was often conflicted regarding his dad. He wondered about the origin of his father's treatment of his mom— was it due to a lack of example or a character flaw? Rob didn't grow up in a household where a healthy marriage relationship was displayed, so how would he know how a good husband was supposed to treat his wife? But there were encouraging moments.

As a child, Pat saw a picture of his dad's barracks from his Navy days. He noticed that while most guys had pictures of pinup girls in their lockers, his father posted a picture of his mom and sister. That image sparked hope for Pat, that perhaps his dad was an honorable man. Pat believed, and later observed, that his dad truly loved his mom, but decided the lack of a good father and husband example to emulate, left his own dad little to model in a healthy way.

Rob Garibay embodied as many positive characteristics as he did negative. Perhaps he was conflicted within himself, as he apparently struggled with many insecurities. Despite having a brilliant mind for designing and problem-solving, Rob had never finished college, and saw that as a failure. He was employed as a sales engineer, but he never let on that he wasn't an engineer with a degree. Rob's feelings of unworthiness became a catalyst for actions he took out on the family, often for no apparent reason. His actions, by today's standards, would be considered abusive—both emotionally and physically. There were very few words of affirmation from Pat's dad for any of his family, which took a toll on everyone. He only engaged the children around activities that he personally enjoyed, and when his kids selected their preferred hobbies, he chose absence or disengagement. Yet Rob's hard work ethic, how he provided for his family, and his expectations of excellence left an indelible impression on his kids that helped each of them when they grew up.

Pat's mom, on the other hand, was a living example of God's love. Despite being an accomplished young woman who could have boasted about her many talents, she chose humility and consistently demonstrated God's forgiving acceptance. She always put family first. Connie's heart remained open and dedicated to family, whether it was Rob's mother, who eventually came to live with the Garibays, his sister's family, or her own brother and his kids. And she gave her all for her children, passing on her deep faith in a loving God and Savior.

These influences shaped Pat's view of family—how important it is for families to be stable, to help one another, and for parents to be tuned into children's needs. Pat believes his dad did the best he could, though his mom and siblings had many unmet emotional needs. Today, Pat is committed to looking to God for the best fatherly example.

When I was in grade school, I had no idea how any of this mattered. Reflecting back however, I see God's providence and care, so evident in His bringing Pat to Cincinnati. Ultimately, my husband became my very best friend. We had so many commonalities. Pat was the third son and I was the third daughter. Our families were of the same size and had similar values, our fathers were both engineers, and each of us had a (sometimes) cruel parent. And we shared the same faith tradition. Our families had both risen beyond a lot of difficulties, and we had become resilient in our approaches to life.

When you look back at your own life, I hope you can see God's hand at work. He places people in your path, some for a season, some for a lifetime, but it's all part of His plan.

Pat and I have marveled over our early beginning. God drew us together at such a young age, often because we understood the difficulties the other endured. I don't claim to comprehend everything about God's provision, but my heavenly Father knew just what His daughter needed then as He does now. Pat was only one candle God sent to drive back the darkness in my life, as I've sometimes been his. And I've only begun to share the miraculous ways our Father has taken care of us.

HAVE YOU CONSIDERED . . .

- *How important are parenting attitudes in the development of one's character identity?*
- *What unique challenges do single parents and their children face?*
- *Do you use your past as an excuse or a motivation?*

CHAPTER SIX

SOULMATES

1971–1973

It was difficult having a disabled father. The day-to-day care was tough, but the hardest part was watching his condition worsen. I could see the heaviness he carried because of the role reversal; his desire was to take care of us, yet we were the ones taking care of him.

There were, however, two bright spots in my junior high years. First, our family was blessed with a surprise baby, my little brother Todd. He quickly became the light of my life. Secondly, I met my soulmate.

I can honestly say I did not have romantic feelings towards Pat when I first met him in third grade, but as I matured, I began seeing attributes I admired. I guess you might say he grew on me. One particularly memorable moment attracted me.

Pat was once again in trouble at school. The teacher made him memorize the longest poem in our literature book. *The Legend of Sherwood Forest* was the most feared "poem punishment" of every student, and none had succeeded in reciting it from memory. When it came time for Pat to stand in front of the class and repeat the poem from memory as his punishment, we were all silent, fearing his fate.

Pat stood up, put his hands in his pockets, and shifted from the left foot to the right. He cleared his throat and started to speak, ever so slowly.

Immediately enthralled, I hung onto Pat's every word, more and more amazed. He recited the poem flawlessly. After he punctuated the final sentence, silence hung in the room, as every student stared wide-eyed at our new hero.

Then the classroom erupted in wild applause. Pat blushed, lowered his head, and walked back to his seat. Not only was I impressed that he managed to memorize a six-page poem, but I also liked the tenacity he showed. I admired that kind of spunk.

Do you remember grade school? There was a whole lot of "who likes who" but not a lot of reality in those "relationships."

Pat and I both remember the first time we felt an undeniable mutual connection. We were at a party during our eighth-grade year. We each stood near a pool table at our friend's house. Pat's bell bottoms and silk shirt with an apache tie marked him as "in style." My color-blocked oversized cardigan, huge hoop earrings, jean flares and platform sandals mimicked outfits I'd seen in teen magazines. Carly Simon's "You're so Vain" and Three Dog Night's "Joy to the World" played over the speakers. I remember the clothes and the music. Pat remembers something different.

Pat says my eyes were what drew him in to conversation with me. "Hey," he said, immediately looking down at his shuffling feet.

"Hi," I said. After a few seconds of awkward silence I added, "Good music, huh."

"Sure." When Pat lifted his gaze back to mine, my pulse quickened. A few stilted words and a mesmerizing stare altered both of our futures.

My heart still melts from that memory. When we got home from the party, Pat called me right away. I don't remember exactly what we talked about, but I remember feeling like I had just met my best friend.

Pat and I started spending time together and talking for hours on the phone each night. I so loved James Taylor's song, *Fire and Rain*. The lyrics about time spent on the telephone summarized our conversations. Often, we talked about the problems we were having at home, but by the time I hung up, Pat's support and encouragement had given me the strength to face another day.

We even began doing our schoolwork together. Some of our assignments consisted of watching filmstrips and listening to audio on a record player in the school's audiovisual room. I must confess, on occasion, instead of listening to the assigned soundtrack, we may have slipped in a Loggins and Messina record. Pat had given me the album, and his sweet gesture tested my strong moral barometer. I thought it respectful to give it a listen, even if that meant interrupting our civics class and bending the rules ever so slightly. You can justify anything when you're in love.

> You can justify anything when you're in love.

It seems every life event during my grade school years was accompanied by a song. Sharing music with friends helped me release emotions and offered an outlet for dreaming about what could be. Little did we know at the time that music was also providing fuel for our thoughts and worldview, and was impacting our values and how we viewed right from wrong.

I started to come into my own during that season. I began recognizing and understanding my gifts while succeeding in escaping my home life. I was no longer a shy girl who sucked her thumb and twirled her hair around her finger. I blossomed into quite the social butterfly, becoming someone who enjoyed her classmates and their friendships. I rarely turned down the opportunity to spend time with people in my peer relationships. They affirmed me and provided a fertile ground where I thrived.

While these positive experiences were occurring, my dad's condition forced him to retire from his job. And though the constant cloud of sadness in my home still hung in the air, Pat and I excitedly talked about our upcoming graduation from the shelter of our small, rural, private grade school. Starting high school made us feel like we were becoming adults, entering a world of hope and new beginnings. Of course, the reality of what seemed like an exciting future would still be colored gray by the storms on the horizon.

HAVE YOU CONSIDERED . . .

- *What characteristics or attributes constitute a soulmate for you?*

- *What was the impact of music on your adolescence?*

- *If you played the highlight reel of your grade school years, what would they look like?*

CHAPTER SEVEN

TEENAGE ANGST

1973–1975

I vividly remember how I felt being a teenaged caretaker for my father. During the day, high school provided an escape and offered hopeful distraction. But my mood shifted as soon as I left school to go home—when harsh reality hit.

As soon as I entered the foyer of our wheelchair-accessible house, I steeled myself for the requests that immediately began. My dad, the man I adored, needed help with even the simplest tasks. A typical afternoon consisted of lighting his pipe, grabbing a snack for him, and having to put my father on the toilet with a Hoyer Lift.

The lift occupied a decent amount of space in his bedroom. It was an assistive device that allowed us to transfer him between his bed and his wheelchair and the toilet. Putting Dad on the toilet was a daily occurrence. First, I pumped the lever connected to the metal rims of a pad he sat on in his wheelchair. His entire frail body was lifted into the air where I steadied him as I slowly swung him over the toilet seat. The anxiety rose in my chest as I did my best to position him just right. I then reversed the lever to lower his body onto the toilet. I did my best not to look him in the eye. After all he had lost, I wanted my dad to at least keep his dignity.

When he finished, I returned to the room, wiped him off, and reversed the process to safely get him back into his wheel-chair. He hated having to ask for this type of help, but you have little choice but to adapt your relationship with someone who is chronically ill. Dad worried that these would be the only memories we would have of him. However, God is so faithful. After his death, these were the first of my memories about Dad to fade.

All of the special moments my dad missed over the years, like the school's father-daughter dances or teaching me how to drive a car, have made my spirit heavy. I know my dad was heartbroken at having to miss so much. But despite his state of debilitation, Dad was always an encourager.

One time, I received a deficiency report in algebra and was mortified as to what my mom would say or do. Dad and I pinky swore, agreeing that Mom would not find out if I promised to be tutored by him to raise my grade. I was thrilled with the remedy and we began our evening tutorials pronto. He was a good listener, and when he did speak, he offered pearls of wisdom and assurances like, "Yesterday is history, tomorrow is a mystery, and today is a gift. That is why it is called the present."

As a teenaged girl, with emotions flitting all over the place, I grew very resentful of my mom because of the way she treated my dad and our family. Reflecting back on the details, I have a better understanding of her frustrations. Dad's electric wheel-chair couldn't be moved easily, so it was kept in my parents' bedroom where it charged every night. Dad's hospital bed had to be raised and lowered regularly. And the Hoyer Lift was always found bedside. None of this created a very romantic setting for a married couple, and Mom relentlessly reminded Dad of "Camelot Lost."

My mother struggled to come to terms with the life we were given. "I had to build this God-awful mausoleum for you," she often screamed. That's what she called our home, "a mausoleum."

"What kind of normal home has to have ramps and all new bathrooms? This wheelchair house will be the death of me! I hate it!" I can only imagine how her words made my father feel.

Because my bedroom was located directly above my parents', I could hear her nightly rants through the vent. It was a constant, vicious cycle. She expressed her frustration and loneliness through rage. Over time, her dependency on alcohol also increased. Manhattans were typically her poison of choice, and many nights she drowned herself in their temporary relief.

Hearing the "clink, clink" of ice against her glass, as she stumbled through our home, alerted me. My stomach turned to knots with every clink at the thought of what would happen next.

Sometimes, she became inebriated to the point of falling. Once, she fell so hard she broke her teeth. I survived the best I could as I watched her spend each evening changing into a woman I no longer knew. There are many moments during my high school years I wish I could erase from my memory completely: my mom's verbal abuse turning physical, her disloyalty to my father, and the times she screamed at the top of her lungs when I disappointed her. These are but a few of the most painful examples seared into my mind.

With each poor choice my mother made, the distance between us grew greater. This distance did not happen because

I understood healthy boundaries or avoiding toxic people. I truly feared her.

After experiencing one of my mom's violent episodes, I confided in Pat. Wiping my eyes and sputtering through angry tears, I said, "I'll never be like my mother."

After listening compassionately, he settled me down and offered words of affirmation and love. "Don't forget, your mom is not all evil. She has a lot of positive attributes, as well." He has always been my safe place, giving me what I needed when everything felt dark.

And Pat was right, there were traits I loved about my mom. She periodically showed a caring nature, generous spirit, and a friendly personality. She wanted the best for her children, a life different from her own. She did not want her kids to suffer the frustration and loneliness she endured and was passionate about all of her children pursuing their unique talents and dreams.

It is bittersweet to think about the dichotomy of my childhood. On one hand, dealing with my mom was difficult and, at times, impossible. But then on the other hand, she displayed random moments of great generosity and kindness.

During my junior year of high school, Mom suggested I take a month-long trip to study at the University of Paris, and she took all the steps to make it happen. That trip was not an easy thing for her financially, but she did it. I developed my love for travel from that experience.

Mom's character shifts caused confusion for me. I constantly had to guess which Mom would show up: the generous, compassionate mom or the one full of anger and frustration who had too much to drink.

Throughout my life, I have learned a lot about identifying and understanding toxic relationships. It is a difficult lesson

It is a difficult lesson for those of us who are "fixers" and believe with just a little positivity and better behavior, people can improve or change, to discover it is not always true.

for those of us who are "fixers" and believe with just a little positivity and better behavior, people can improve or change, to discover it is not always true.

I remember hearing this message for the first time at an Alcoholics Anonymous meeting I attended with my sister. The moderator surprised me when she said, "Your mother's condition is not your fault."

I also learned that all the personal behavior modifications I attempted, and in guilt took on, would never result in my mom getting better. She had to make the decision to change, it was totally up to her.

WOW! What a concept. Personal responsibility despite your circumstances. Consistency despite your emotions. Self-control. Reliability. What an epiphany!

These qualities remind me of the Lord I serve. He is faithful, reliable, consistent, unchanging, never-ending, always available, ever positive, and the bright morning star lighting my life.

I pray you know God like this. Despite the pain we humans can extol on one another, the Lord can redeem it. He can redeem you.

God's love is perfect, and it completes us, filling the voids that may be left from another's abuse. The need to renew one's mind is a daily undertaking that requires prayer, grace, and the self-discipline of filling yourself with regular reminders of

God's truth, found in the Bible. The beauty of the Lord is that He longs to comfort His children, all we must do is ask. I've had to do it through every stage of my life. Maybe you will relate to some of my experiences.

HAVE YOU CONSIDERED . . .

- *When in your life have you had to draw healthy boundaries to protect your mental well-being?*

- *Have you ever found yourself feeling responsible for another person's bad choices due to guilt?*

- *What does it mean in Romans 12:2 when it says to "be transformed by the renewing of your mind"? Why is this so important?*

CHAPTER EIGHT

CHECKLIST

1975–1977

Aren't first dates awkward? Ours sure was. Although, to this day, it is still one of my favorite memories.

Pat, with the help of his twelve-hour-old driver's license, took me to the Red and White Dance on February 22, 1975. We had dinner at Schuller's Wigwam Restaurant beforehand, a popular spot in a suburb of Cincinnati. Pat ordered lobster for the first time in his life, but he acted cool and mature as if he was a seasoned, professional lobster connoisseur.

He did a nice job of pulling the meat out of the shell, and I pretended not to see the side glance he gave me to make sure I was checking him out. But as he proceeded to dip the lobster into the butter dish, his overconfidence caused a distinctive PLOP. The lobster slipped into the dish, spilling butter all over the table. So much for being cool. We laughed at his failed lobster-eating demonstration all the way to the dance. It was a great beginning.

Laughing became the bedrock of our relationship and our shared joy continued as we dated throughout our high school years. Pat went to LaSalle, an all-boy Catholic high school, and I went to McAuley, LaSalle's all-girl counterpart. Despite neither of us having an example of a healthy relationship, loving each other seemed to come naturally.

We went to all the school dances together and saw each other every weekend. Pat found plenty of reasons to come to McAuley, and I loved seeing him unexpectedly during the school day. Every now and then, despite my rule-following ways, we snuck a kiss when the nuns weren't looking. Pat kept me on my toes and pushed me beyond my comfort limits. I loved it.

Pat continuously intrigued me. In some ways we were similar, but our differences made us want to learn more about each other. He was a logical guy who enjoyed science and math—everything had its place—and life fit together like puzzle pieces. I, on the other hand, leaned toward literature and theatre and was a bit of a dreamer by nature.

So, I started to dream. What would it feel like to be married to Pat Garibay? Even though I would ponder it more seriously later, I was already formulating my checklist. Pat fared well.

√ Hard worker

√ Solution minded

√ Handy

√ Strong sense of right and wrong

√ Easy to talk to

√ Loves kids

√ Helps with my dad and respects him

√ Passionate about good causes

√ Tall, dark, and handsome

This guy would make a great husband someday, I thought to myself on several occasions. At the very least, he was someone I wanted to seriously date. He was the complete package and it was clear he loved me. It warmed my heart to know he wanted to be with me so much. But had I understood my identity in Christ at the time, I would not have had such a strong desire for another person's love and acceptance. I had not yet learned about the abundance of unconditional love that the Lord was waiting to pour into my thirsty soul. If I had, the times Pat and I were at odds would not have been as hard as they were.

> Had I understood my identity in Christ at the time, I would not have had such a strong desire for another person's love and acceptance.

At risk of painting too rosy a picture of my relationship with Pat, the truth is, there are some painful memories as well. We've experienced a lot of stretching and growing. Over the years, we've had disagreements and moments of "the silent treatment." At times, the grass appeared greener and we questioned our decision to be together. But we stuck it out and decided early on to fight for one another and our commitment. We've repeatedly chosen to love, even when it was not easy.

As a couple now in their fortieth year of marriage, it is funny and heartwarming to reflect on our youthful perspectives and actions. Our relationship resolve has helped it grow over all these decades. One thing we are sure of, our love never would have lasted this long without the adoration of our heavenly Father and His guidance throughout our marriage.

In high school, Pat continually caused trouble—though honestly, he did not see himself as a troublemaker, just a jokester who enjoyed pranking people. Perhaps some folks did not appreciate his sense of humor, but he was authentic nonetheless.

Pat was cool, well dressed, athletic, smart, and had hair longer than mine. But amongst all his predictably attractive traits, he also belonged to his school's chess club. I loved that about him. His involvement in that pastime showed a complex side to his personality, spotlighting his insatiable desire to solve problems and understand the world. He really didn't care if people thought he was a nerd by being part of this club. Pat just loved the game, and frankly, he enjoyed the company of the guys with whom he competed.

Pat will be the first to admit that during his teen years, his pride began to rear its head as he realized he could do almost anything he set his mind to. It was also at this time in his life he questioned how God engaged with the decisions he made. Despite living without leaning on Christ, Pat knew God existed but did not understand that He cared about the details of his life.

Another one of Pat's favorable traits was his love for people and his great compassion for them. He knew his future would include a vocation of impact, but he was unsure what that might look like—or how his choices would influence me.

Besides my relationship with Pat, high school brought other adventures. I was a member of the theatrical club and active in several school productions. I was very comfortable on stage and loved immersing myself into a variety of characters. Because of this, I never developed the common fear of public speaking, and my role-playing fulfilled my desire to live a different life. I saw my life as reflective of the comedy/

tragedy masks which typically symbolize theater. As an actor, these masks were readily available for my use, dependent on my mood or situation.

On the outside, I was a happy girl, but I carried secrets inside that I did not easily share. My tendency to slip into a make-believe world, coupled with the sadness of watching my dad's health decline and listening to my mother's rants, opened the door to melancholy. Our family never talked about handling depression, and many days I fought this battle on my own.

Daily thoughts ran through my head. *I'm a performer. I can portray a different persona. I can be anyone I want to be. No one needs to see how I really feel.* I put on the comedy mask just to get through, even though the tragedy mask reared its sad face below the surface of what most others could see.

I started writing poetry, which exposed my pain and proved to be a cathartic outlet. I was not sure I could verbalize my depression, but I could write about it. Over time, the masks I wore did not prove emotionally or mentally sustainable, but my journals provided a place where I could be authentic.

While I struggled, I didn't have a lot of girlfriends, but I did have Jane. Jane was a "safe friend." She understood me, shared my interests in social injustice and politics, but more importantly, she knew about my dad. So, we hung out at Jane's house much of the time—it was lighthearted and fun there. Her family was tight knit, had parties, told stories, and played games. They felt alive. I wanted to feel alive, too. Their influence in my life created a blueprint for the family I wanted one day.

Finally, Pat and I made it to our senior year. We were on the cusp of making the first major decision of our lives. College was about to begin, and I was sure it would bring with it the life I always wanted. But the next chapter proved to be one of the most difficult I'd experienced yet.

HAVE YOU CONSIDERED . . .

- *What are the ideal attributes of a friend, spouse, or parent? How do these ideals compare to the attributes of Christ?*

- *Christ cares about the intimate details of your life. Have you included Him in your plans for the future?*

- *Why does being untrue to your authentic-self lead to depression?*

CHAPTER NINE

THE UNEXPECTED

1977–1979

I was the first of my siblings to go away to college. Despite my relocation to Columbus, Ohio, I was still unable to release the guilty feelings of leaving my family and the situation at home. Although I tried to make weekly phone calls to my parents to soothe my soul, my true comfort came from being at school with Pat. We both had dreams and goals we wanted to achieve. Since he was a young boy, Pat had planned to become a veterinarian, and I was wavering between becoming an attorney or a teacher.

No matter the career path I chose, I knew Pat was the man I would marry. Our love for one another had grown so strong that we could not deny the desire to be as close as possible. One weekend when we went home to visit our parents, Pat spoke to his dad about our hopes of a soon-to-occur wedding. We had a brilliant idea, as nineteen-year-olds often do, to save money on room and board by getting married and living together. In his wisdom, Pat's dad discouraged the plan and encouraged us to continue as we already were—dating and focused on school.

Despite our failed plan, our passion for one another did not decrease. We mentally and emotionally pledged ourselves to one another and felt certain it would just be a matter of time before we formalized our marriage by vows and law. Because of this mindset and our lack of scriptural understanding, we made choices that greatly affected our future.

> Because of this mindset and our lack of scriptural understanding, we made choices that greatly affected our future.

Prior to our sophomore year, I began battling nausea in the mornings. After missing two of my regular cycles, we came to terms with the thought that I might be pregnant. We felt it necessary to get confirmation.

It was a rainy, overcast day, and the twenty-minute drive to the Planned Parenthood clinic in Cincinnati felt like it took hours. I couldn't imagine what I was going to do. My life was whirling by, as though I had to figure out every detail on the way to the clinic. Thoughts swirled in my mind. *If I am pregnant, I will be disappointing everyone in my life. All of my career dreams will be gone.*

Sitting in the waiting room with Pat, looking at the worn, dog-eared magazines on the rack, I felt like that scared little girl I thought I had left behind. I clutched Pat's hand, thankful that the only man in the room was mine. Looking around, I wondered what was going through the minds of the other young women dressed in their bell bottoms and polo shirts. Each gazed into oblivion or immersed themselves into pamphlets on women's health—pretending to absorb the type of information no one really wanted to read.

The room was filled with deafening silence and smelled medicinal. It lacked any sense of warmth and hospitality. The environment felt cold and impersonal. A sign hung on the wall read, *Every child a wanted child.* My heart leapt upon reading that message.

I wanted our child, as it was the manifestation of our love. But we had not planned our parenthood very well. At the time, I wasn't familiar with the extent of medical practices the clinic participated in—we were simply drawn in by the free pregnancy test.

The door opened and my name was called. I could not breathe. My heart raced and my surroundings spun. I sensed my future was going to be decided in the next few moments. I followed the nurse—I think she was a nurse—into a small, sterile office and she proceeded to sit down behind her desk. She robotically pulled out a manila folder and started flipping through the pages, never engaging with my worried eyes.

She leaned back and the chair squeaked. I watched her . . . waiting.

"Well, the test is positive. You are ten weeks pregnant."

It sounded like someone hit a clanging symbol. I saw her lips move, but I couldn't hear a word.

In a monotone voice, she said, "Patti?"

I blinked, "Yes! Yes, what? Do you need something else from me?"

"Well," she said, "I want to make sure you know you have options. Given your age and obvious single status, I recommend an abortion. We can go ahead and schedule that for you. When is a good time?" She scanned a calendar on her clipboard nonchalantly, then finally stopped to look at me.

She continued, "Patti? Do you want to go ahead and schedule that while I have the calendar in front of me?"

The year was 1978 and as a woman who was just starting to find my own voice, I had a choice to make. *Is this baby just a nuisance I can easily choose to be rid of?* No, abortion was clearly wrong. *Do I seek God now? I wish I would have thought of that earlier.* The inner dialogue continued quickly in my mind, but I eventually heard myself speak.

"No." I said. "If we're done here, I'd like to leave."

The clinic worker nodded slowly and said, "I understand. This is a tough decision." She reached across the desk to try to pat my hand, but I stood up and put my hands in the pockets of my jeans. "Trust me," she said, as she rolled back in her chair, "The sooner you schedule the appointment, the easier it is to take care of."

With that, I left her office and somehow navigated my way out to the lobby. Pat and I, holding hands, walked out of the clinic together. On the walk to the car, we remained silent. As soon as we were both in the car, I sobbed and fell into his arms. "The test was positive," I sputtered.

He did not seem surprised. He soothed my hair and kissed my lips and assured me, "It will all be okay."

I was not as sure.

Prior to this appointment, we both agreed that abortion was not a viable option for us. Despite the 1973 passage of *Roe v. Wade*, the landmark decision of the U.S. Supreme Court to legalize abortion, we went against the cultural norms and chose life. We decided to take the next right step with whatever consequences might come. We walked out of the Planned Parenthood clinic and never looked back. I was nineteen years old, and while I was not sure what the future trajectory of our life might look like, I knew that taking the life of a child to fit my imagined Camelot was not an option.

Finding out I was pregnant was a wake-up call. Pat and I lived in shock for a couple of days, and then he took the initiative. "We need to back up. We can handle this together. But right now, under these circumstances, marriage is not the right decision for us. We should not get married until we have clearer minds."

"What? That's the first thing we're going to do," I argued.

How can this be happening? How can the love of my life now decide getting married is off the table?

I totally disagreed, but Pat wanted to wait, and, in the whirling clouds of uncertainty, I tried to hear him out.

"Patti, I am sure we will eventually get married."

Eventually was not the word I wanted to hear.

He continued, "I don't want a shotgun wedding. Marriage, from all I have seen, is tough enough. Too many couples are getting divorced, and I don't want us to get married because we 'had' to."

Of course, his theory made sense to a logical, strategically thinking guy—but to me? I felt abandoned and alone. Single motherhood was not on my list of future goals.

We knew at this point we had to tell our families. It was an emotional discussion with my parents, Pat at my side. The disappointment on my father's face haunted me for years. I knew the disappointment was not because he was upset with me, but because he was sad for me. Life would be tough, and that was not the life he had hoped for me to have.

And then the questions began: "Well, what are you guys going to do about it? Are you getting married? Where are you going to live? Are you quitting school?" The peppering of questions seemed endless.

Pat and I explained that we would not be getting married right away. I did wonder, and I am sure my family also did, if he was running away from his obligation.

Pat spared me the embarrassment of telling his parents. He told them on his own. He barely remembers their reaction. Emotions were so high, and we were filled with anxiety. In life, difficult times like these are often hard to recall.

One unfortunate memory has never left my mind, however. My aunt's words when she learned I was pregnant hit me hard. "You were special. You were going to do great things and now THIS!"

Her words felt like daggers that made my heart sink. My aunt was my godmother and we were very close. I knew she was yet another person I had let down. I always struggled with low self-esteem and now I felt as though I had nothing left to cling to that brought me any amount of worth.

We lived the next months, day by day, seemingly hour by hour. I thought if we were meant to be together, we'd be together. But all I could do was wait. It was tough, because I was still unsure of Pat's true intentions. I trusted him, yet my insecurities bubbled up, and I often questioned my own judgment. I was nineteen, pregnant, unsure of school, and uncertain if I would get married. I decided to stay with my sister Karen for a few weeks to clear my head and try to make sense of my broken life.

I didn't know what to expect in my pregnancy. It wasn't like my mom was excited to come alongside me to share her experience and lessons learned. Everything was scary and new, and I truly felt like Hester Prynne of Nathaniel Hawthorne's *The Scarlet Letter*. The pregnancy should have been jubilant and exciting, but I felt sinful and dirty. I faced this time somewhat alone, as though it was my duty to pay for our mistake.

In retrospect, I wish I would have known the power of going to the Lord in prayer. But because I was not yet in a relationship with Christ, the thought of talking to Him about my problems and hurts was not my natural inclination. My self-reliance reigned supreme and I committed to make this time as joyful and memorable as possible.

Pat and I eventually moved in together, living in the up-stairs of Pat's elderly coworker's home. Again, due to our lack of biblical guidance, we thought this made sense as we continued to make decisions using our limited knowledge rather than God's infinite wisdom. At that time, Pat was working two jobs while I tackled a full-time class load at the University of Cincinnati. I think I was trying to underscore my worth by keeping my academic dreams moving forward.

Late in my pregnancy, I knew something was off. I had a sharp rise in blood pressure, my hands, feet, and face swelled, and I endured incredibly intense headaches. I was diagnosed with a severe case of toxemia. All I could do was sit and wait during a hospital stay that lasted almost a month. While my shame grew in public display, my body struggled to recover.

Through it all, Pat offered amazing support. He was my constant visitor, bringing me flowers he found in the dump-ster behind the funeral home next to our apartment. In prepa-ration for our child's arrival, he practiced serving as my most dedicated birthing coach while I convalesced.

As my due date inched closer, we took Lamaze classes to-gether where we learned what to expect. Without Pat, I could not have endured the labor. He encouraged me, dabbed my forehead with a cool cloth, held my hand, rubbed my back, encouraged me to keep my focal point, and kept telling me to breathe. I was dedicated to giving birth naturally without the commonly used epidural. But I did not consider the length of a first labor nor the intensity of the pain, particularly because my labor had to be induced via Pitocin. I may have reconsidered my heroic efforts if I had known what lay ahead of me.

After twenty hours of what seemed to be neverending labor, the room filled with medical professionals. We were informed that the baby was coming—ready or not. Pat had to leave and scrub up, and then wait to be called in for reentry to the delivery room. Unfortunately, they did not call him in time, and after all those hours of grueling labor, Pat missed seeing the birth of his first child. He tears up to this day when he thinks of missing that once in a lifetime moment.

We chose the name Rachael—it means "ewe" or "lamb" in Hebrew. Little did we know at the time what a fitting name it was for our precious firstborn.

Following Rachael's arrival, I was naïve enough to believe all my fears, anxieties, and shame would melt away, now that I was a mom. What a gift this child was. Her miraculous entrance into the world prompted my soul to give thanks to the Creator for His provision and the safe arrival of this bundle of joy.

Seeing my precious daughter's face, nursing her after delivery, and holding her tiny, clenched fists melted my heart and changed my life. Rachael completed Pat and me as a family and knitted our hearts together, forever.

With the help of friends, we moved back to Columbus to attend Ohio State University in the spring of 1979. Childcare, limited finances, time pressures, caring for three versus one, and a full class load made college quite challenging. Our parents expected us to continue our educations, and we did not want to let them down—again. We adjusted, learned, and began to develop our new life together.

Pat and I were married on September 15, 1979, when Rachael was six months old. In preparation, we attended pre-marriage counseling to help ready us for this lifelong commitment. We were fortunate that the priests who both counseled and married us were family friends. Their support and love were such a blessing. Looking back, the Lord provided exactly what we needed at that time in our lives.

Reflecting on these memories fills my eyes with tears. It has been quite a while since I opened this vault of emotion. I am overwhelmed by God's faithfulness and His love for me, even when I barely acknowledged Him. Since then, I've learned so much about His patience and unconditional love for us.

In the middle of my mess ups, I felt worthless, but God saw worth. He placed a burden of truth in both Pat and my hearts that would not allow us to make a decision we would definitely regret. Rather, we took a detour that diverted our desires.

God trusted me to be the mother of a beautiful girl, and He knew Pat would be an amazing father. He patiently waited for us to confess our sins and make decisions; He never forced us. He knew we would ultimately seek Him. Now, as I look back, I am reminded of 1 John 1:9. It says, *If we confess our sins, He is faithful and just to forgive us our sins and purify us from all unrighteousness.* Of course, I would need that faithful promise again.

HAVE YOU CONSIDERED . . .

- *Why is it important to understand that what is acceptable culturally is not always acceptable to God?*

- *When confronted with a life-changing decision, where do you immediately go for guidance?*

- *In accordance with 1 John 1:9, when you make a mistake, are you able to humble yourself and repent? Are you willing to accept the grace and mercy the Lord provides through His forgiveness and restoration?*

CHAPTER TEN

UNLIKELY AVENUES

1981–1984

A leaking roof, chipping paint, a crying baby, and two broke newlywed college kids using food stamps to buy their groceries—that was us. This was a rough period for our newly formed family. In addition to both of us going to school full-time, Pat had a part-time job. But our schedule was simply not sustainable and our bills unpayable.

Pat's brother, Rob, had just started a business as an independent Amway distributor for health and cleaning products. The multilevel business model allowed its successful distributers to earn a good living. Despite Pat's dad calling this "a pyramid scheme," Pat decided to give it a whirl, hoping for some much-needed extra income.

Imagine a long-haired, platform-shoe-wearing, poverty stricken twenty-one-year-old, trying to show others how to become rich. Little did we know how this unlikely opportunity would influence our future.

During this time, we learned we were expecting our second child. We were so joyful about the news, yet we had to make some hard choices in regard to our future. After much consideration, Pat dropped out of college with a humbled heart. Along with the fear of being perceived as a failure, he made a huge sacrifice for our family when he gave up his dream of becoming a veterinarian.

Pat continued working full-time throughout my second pregnancy. I did my best to continue my schoolwork and care for our sweet Rachael. When the day of our second child's birth finally came, the timing was unfortunate. Pat was out on a run when my water broke.

After he returned, Pat found me standing in the living room, crying, distraught over having just soaked through the only pair of pants that still fit me. Regardless, off we went to the hospital. A few hours later, we welcomed our dark haired, almond-eyed Meghan.

Pat's efforts were paying off. After having to scrimp and save for so long, we were excited to buy our very first home on the west side of Columbus for a mere $29,000. Despite a less than choice location, the home had character and space for our growing family.

Pat was quick to add personal touches to the house, complete with a picket fence built out of leftover pallets. This addition to our backyard allowed us to tolerate our new, rambunctious pup, Nicki, a little more.

I loved that little backyard, particularly because it contained a cherry tree just like the one from my childhood. I couldn't wait to bake a pie for my husband. Unfortunately, my adored fruit tree proved to be a better bird feeder than cherry provider. Trying to help, Pat climbed the tree to hang pie pans in the branches, hoping to scare the birds away. As he was tying them in the highest part of the tree, a few birds brazenly swooped in and landed. They ate several prized cherries right in front of him. That year, our harvest yielded enough fruit for just one pie, but boy, was it good.

Right behind the house, Pat assembled a small plastic pool for the girls to enjoy on hot summer days. Some evenings, we all attempted to fit into that tiny pool, giggling and splashing the whole time. We may not have had much in the way of possessions, but I loved seeing my children's pleasure from small, everyday activities.

Our next-door neighbors became good friends with the girls and spent endless hours playing in our very hot third-floor attic. Often, the kids reappeared with sweat dripping down their faces. As a local Kool-Aid mom, I took care of their thirst. Nothing pleased me more than being Pat's wife and the mother of our two kids. I loved being referred to as "the Garibays."

Now with two daughters under the age of three, I felt compelled to leave school and become a full-time mom. Although I only had student teaching left to complete my bachelor of science degree in secondary education, money was non-existent for childcare. Mine seemed to be the right decision. My dreams of earning a degree needed to be put on hold.

Pat was still working his Amway business on the side and felt it important that we attend an Amway convention in Michigan. The organization's leadership team seemed amazing to us. They were good people, family-oriented, successful, and appeared to have a faith that gave them inner strength. We wanted to be like them.

At the convention, we attended the Sunday worship service that was always part of an Amway conference and listened to the sermon intently. At the end of his message, the preacher gave an altar call for the twenty thousand-plus attendees. To my surprise, in reaction, Pat walked down from the upper level of the arena. My husband gave his life to the Lord that day.

Nothing stayed the same after that. Faith ignited Pat and became the guide of his life. He developed an insatiable hunger for Scripture and determined to become the godly dad his precious daughters needed and deserved.

We've since learned that while educational and career pursuits are valid goals to have in order to provide for your family, they are temporal and pale in comparison to the light of eternity. Had we not left college at the time we did, Pat would have missed his opportunity at Amway, the door that ultimately led to his salvation. That choice made him understand the nature of his heavenly Father, allowing him to become the best dad possible.

> While educational and career pursuits are valid goals to have in order to provide for your family, they are temporal and pale in comparison to the light of eternity.

Prior to this time, we attended the neighborhood Catholic church. We dedicated ourselves to this local parish, helping where we could. The church did not have a room to take your young children to if they cried. It really bothered me, because it was so difficult to pray and feel part of the mass with two toddlers hanging on my sleeve. But I didn't want to just complain about the problem, so I offered to create a solution. I spoke with the priest about starting a preschool or a nursery program for the parish. I was more than willing to lead this initiative and was so disappointed when he expressed no interest in pursuing the idea. It was then I knew our attendance would be short lived.

Pat's brother attended a Church of the Nazarene in Michigan at this time, which gave us the idea to investigate one in our area. As I looked in the Yellow Pages for a church with a nursery program, I hoped to find one in the same denomination. We discovered Warren Avenue Church of the Nazarene, just a few streets away from our home.

We visited the church a few times and felt welcomed. Pastor Vernon and his wife, Norma, were straight from West Virginia. He used a fire-and-brimstone style of preaching—very different for two Catholics. Yet, he and his precious wife had pure hearts of warmth and compassion. We quickly came to love the biblical teaching of our new church and the family atmosphere it provided.

On any given Sunday, you could hear the piano playing from outside as you walked up the crumbled steps to enter the vestibule. It was a beautiful, old stone building, with stained glass windows, original woodwork, and traditional red-fabric pews with Bibles in the wooden pockets.

After we became more comfortable with attending services there, Vernon and Norma asked to share a meal with us. They were much older, and we considered them our spiritual parents. In fact, everyone at that church was probably thirty-five years older than we were, but many of those people invested in our spiritual walk. Soon, we joined a small group and began forming bonds with other members. The people in that congregation taught us the importance of having solid Christian friends. Proverbs 27:17 reminds us, *As iron sharpens iron, so one person sharpens another.* Never did we expect an older couple from the hills of West Virginia to touch our lives so profoundly.

Before long, Pastor Vernon offered me a part-time job as the church secretary. I didn't know how to use any of the equipment necessary for the role but I took the job, working two days a week. I learned quickly and eagerly. Being involved at the church helped our spiritual lives blossom even more.

Pat continued to take his role as the faith leader of our family very seriously. I was still a bit behind Pat regarding my spiritual walk. I vacillated between setting correct priorities and trying to understand grace, though I was most curious about what it meant to be a true, biblical Christian.

Pat wanted to get baptized to show an outward commitment to the Lord's position as Master of his life. I shared that desire, so in May 1983, we got baptized together. I knew I had room to grow in the faith department and needed to invest time into its development, however, the Lord soon intervened in my heart. New lessons were coming. The next trial in our lives highlighted the importance of faith over fear when our world becomes shaken to its core.

HAVE YOU CONSIDERED . . .

- *Has God ever used an unlikely opportunity to bring you great blessings?*

- *Have you had times in your life where you placed your personal goals ahead of your spiritual health?*

- *Do the people you spend your time with encourage your spiritual walk? Have you ever discounted wisdom from another, due to their age and upbringing?*

Pat's parents—Rob and Connie, WWII

Norm and Jean on their wedding day 1953

Norm in Okinawa 1955

Jean and Mary Sue yearning for Norm 1955

Haverkos sisters in Boston 1963

Pat and Patti 3rd Grade—the year we met 1968

Pat's family photo 1967

Patti's family photo 1972

*Pat and Patti in high
school 1976*

*Norm and Patti on Patti's
wedding day 1979*

Pat and Rachael at the hospital 1983

C.R.Y.

C.R.Y.

Caring
Responsibly
for our
Youth

C.R.Y.

P.O. Box 18962
Fairfield, Ohio 45018-0962
(513) 779-3757

C.R.Y. brochure 1994

GREAT RIVERS GIRL SCOUT COUNCIL, INC.
4930 Cornell Rd, Cinti, OH 45242-1884
1-513-489-1025 or 1-800-537-6241

sexuality & you

A weekend retreat for Cadette Girl Scouts
(grades 7-8) to help increase their knowledge,
enhance their self-esteem, and help them
identify their own values in the area of
sexuality.

GIRL SCOUTS

November 5-7, 1993
January 14-16, 1994
February 4-6, 1994
March 11-13, 1994

The innocuous
invitation—1994

Garibay photo circa 1997

Pat and Patti as guests of My Family Talk—
Dr. James Dobson, our parenting mentor 2010

Patti and Jean—2018

Garibay family photo 2019

CHAPTER ELEVEN

A MIRACLE

1983

Our young family fell into our version of normalcy, enjoying our humble home, attending Bible study, and raising our two precious daughters. We started listening to Christian radio, which made a huge impact on our understanding of parenting and living out our faith. Dr. Dobson's *Focus on the Family* program was instrumental to our philosophy of raising children.

Pat received news that his company was opening an office in Cincinnati and wanted him to lead the effort. It was a great opportunity for our family financially, and we loved the idea of returning home. With great anticipation, we headed back to our home town to begin our search for our new house, while Pat's parents watched Rachael and Meghan.

Under the supervision of Pat's Dad and Mom, our four-year-old, Rachael, was playing in the front yard with the children who lived next door to my in-laws. They twirled and swung badminton racquets through the air, making a WHIP sound. Suddenly, the raucous laughter ceased, and a deadly silence hung in the air. One of the playmate's racquets inadvertently hit Rachael in her temple. Her little body fell to the driveway concrete. She was knocked unconscious.

Already on the scene, my mother-in-law rushed to Rachael's side and quickly employed her nursing skills. My daughter soon woke up, and Pat's mom checked her for all the typical signs of head trauma. She kept Rachael by her side for the rest of the day.

When Pat and I returned from house hunting and heard the news, we examined Rachael ourselves and believed she was fine. Her eyes dilated normally, and she was able to stay awake and alert, so all seemed well.

A day later, back home in Columbus, Rachael and Pat were playfully wrestling as they always did near bedtime. However, this time something different took place.

Rachael began vomiting and convulsing. Although I was no stranger to vomiting children, I had never witnessed convulsions before. It seemed that someone else was in control of my daughter's body. Reacting quickly and in a panic, we scooped Meghan from her bed and headed to the emergency room, as Rachael's body continued to react violently.

While we sped to the hospital, it felt like the distance increased instead of shortened with each passing landmark, and the trip was neverending. I wondered, *should we have called an ambulance? Will it matter if we get her there in one minute, two minutes, or ten minutes?* No one on the streets seemed to care that we had an emergency. It felt surreal to hold my child, who was seizing, when the world outside of my car window went on as though nothing was happening.

We finally arrived at the hospital, and Rachael was rushed into the examination room. The medical staff performed tests while Pat, Meghan, and I sat anxiously in the waiting area. Little two-year-old Meghan whimpered quietly as her head lay on my lap, worried about her big sister. We prayed. We worried. We felt alone.

Finally, a doctor came through the door to where we were seated. I noticed him scanning the room and I jumped up, rushing over to him with Pat close behind, holding Meghan.

The doctor showed us back to our seats and crouched down closely, before offering a whispered message. "I don't have a lot of news. But I do know we'll have to admit her to a room in the neurosurgery unit."

I watched the doctor's lips move as he mouthed the words, "Your daughter appears to have a cerebral hematoma on the front left quadrant of her brain. Its location deems it inoperable."

We were in Columbus all by ourselves, with no relatives and only our church family for support. Our tiny, sweet Rachael lay in an oversized hospital bed with an inoperable hematoma the size of a golf ball in her head. We were young, alone, scared, in debt, and now a doctor was telling us this incomprehensible news.

"What do you mean inoperable?" The words slowly tumbled from my tongue as hot tears stung my eyes.

The doctor followed with the scariest words I had ever heard. "If I try to perform surgery, Rachael will not be the same child you know."

My heart jumped into my throat and my chest tightened. I struggled to catch my next breath. Finally managing to gather my thoughts, I asked, "What are our options? We have to have options. We can't just sit here." I have always thought a problem meant it was my responsibility to find a solution.

He said, "She needs observation for twenty-four hours."

Be still and know that I am God. Focus on Psalm 46:10. Those words resounded in my mind.

My worrisome thoughts continued. *Observation? Meaning we have to just watch and wait? Watch her have seizures? Watch her struggle to breathe? Watch her stare blankly? Just be still?* That was an impossible request for me.

But there was nothing I could do. Once they moved Rachael to the twenty-four-hour observation room, I stayed for a while to be with her. There was one nurse to two patients. The other patient was a twelve-year-old boy who was unresponsive, intubated, and on a ventilator. He was a quadriplegic, and in my mommy brain, I thought, *that's what's going to happen to my child.* I could feel my heart slowly shatter as I watched him breathe in and out through the tubes in his throat.

Pat spent the night so I could take baby Meghan home. Rachael continued to have seizures through the night. She was just a little thing with big blue eyes and long, thick, blonde hair. A bright child, she had just been accepted into early kindergarten. She was sweet, loving, and loyal—there seemed to be only goodness and compassion in her heart. We loved her with a love that defied comprehension. How could this possibly happen to her?

We continued the grueling wait for Rachael to be released from the hospital. During her month-long stay, our families visited from Cincinnati, offering their love and support. Pastor Vernon and Norma, along with many other members of our congregation, either came to the hospital and prayed, or prayed wherever they were. One thing remained consistent. We prayed. And we prayed. And we prayed.

The folks from the church offered so many acts of care for our family. In addition to their intercessory prayers, they brought comfort food and sent gifts as well as flowers and

> The love we received from our Christian friends reflected the agape love of God I was learning about through the preacher's sermons.

cards of encouragement. I am so grateful we found this church prior to Rachael's accident. The love we received from our Christian friends reflected the agape love of God I was learning about through the preacher's sermons.

Rachael had angiograms and every intrusive test imaginable. I saw my sweet, now strong child endure intravenous therapy (IV) and daily blood draws. Time moved slowly. I could barely stand the sight of her young body in the huge mechanical bed.

In order to control the seizing, Rachael was put on so many different steroids that she blew up like a round balloon. The steroids were meant to simply alleviate pain and stop the seizures by lowering the pressure on her brain. The doctors really didn't know what else to do.

While our daughter healed, we became friends with the children on that floor. It was heartbreaking to see the vast number of kids who had brain damage, brain cancer, and shunts. Rachael was so loving, accepting all the kids, despite some of their different appearances and abilities. She continued to smile and wait. She was far more patient than me.

My stomach turned every time I walked into the Columbus Children's Hospital. Upon entering its doors, I dreaded the antiseptic smell mixed with the scent of overcooked cafeteria food. But most of all, I dreaded the thought of my poor baby in this sterile place, not in her pretty room at home, eating her favorite foods, playing her board games, and riding her bike.

Amidst this unwanted situation, we tried to make her hospital room as cheery as we could, decorating it with posters and hand-drawn pictures from her friends. Rachael collected smelly stickers and placed them in her sticker books. She clung to her favorite stuffed animal, "Lambie," while she endured daily pokes and pricks and tests. We made a lot of visits to the playroom, IV poles in tow, for puzzles and games and to visit with other precious patients.

The worst part for me was leaving her at night. I tried to be brave for her as we walked out of her room, but as soon as we were out of sight, my emotions erupted the whole way home.

During the time Rachael was in the hospital, I tried to alleviate anxiety by playing with Meghan and cleaning the house. As I tidied Rachael's room one day, I stopped and looked at the name plaque over her bed. In pink words, it read *Rachael—little lamb*. The emptiness of the bed, covered by her quilt spread smoothly across the sheets, was like someone announcing over a P.A. system, "She's not here!"

I pushed through the pain of the moment and continued my chores downstairs, only to be met with another unbearable memory. We had huge, floor-to-ceiling windows in our living room, and I recalled how Rachael would go to the front porch and peek through the windows, waving to me. She'd shout, "Hi Mommy," as I went about my regular cleaning. I wondered if I'd ever experience that kind of beautiful moment again. I wondered if I would ever see her wave to me from the other side of the glass again.

My whole life, I had struggled with guilt and shame, blaming myself for my poor decisions. Once again, I wondered and struggled. Was God upset with me and would Rachael pay for my mistakes? I asked God, "Do we have to offer this little lamb as a sacrifice for our sins? Is that what has to happen?"

The fact of the matter was, we made mistakes in our youth, but Pat and I had both asked Jesus to forgive us of our sins. By His power, our past was redeemed. But at that time, though I clung to my faith, I was still human. I believed God, but still questioned whether I'd missed something.

Finally, after a month of daily updates with the doctors, along with a battery of tests, a neurologist and his team walked into Rachael's room. The bewildered looks on their faces gave me pause.

"Is everything okay?" I said, worried they had found something on a recent MRI. I hoped there wasn't an issue even more devastating than what we had already endured.

The physicians looked at one another, shaking their heads. Our doctor finally spoke, smiling as he said, "We don't know what's going on. There is no medical explanation I can give you, but it's gone. The inoperable hematoma is gone, and we can't explain it."

What amazing news! Accepting it quickly, we notified our prayer chain and they erupted with praise and thanks. The physicians wanted us to sign a release, so they could use Rachael's protocol for a case study because they did not understand how this had happened. We agreed to sign their release, but we knew how and why it had taken place.

Rachael's miracle was a result of God's grace and the power of prayer. During the month of her hospitalization, I finally committed my life wholly to Jesus Christ. I made a deal with God saying, "I will give you anything, including my entire life, if you will only save our Rachael."

God completely healed Rachael. She had no lingering effects from the hematoma. And I kept my commitment to love the Great Physician with my whole heart and my whole soul, even though I didn't really know what true surrender meant yet. I understood it wasn't about literally giving everything away, but was about receiving everything because you were willing to give it away. One thing I was clear about—my life was no longer mine, it was simply a life on loan.

It's so ironic. The precious baby born out of wedlock, whose name means "little lamb," was given back to us. We didn't deserve this outcome, but we were full of gratitude.

This difficult and scary situation made a profound impression on me. I began to see a glimpse of what God wanted me to do and believed I was capable of, even though for so long, I had felt unworthy. I had listened to the lies of the enemy who told me I wasn't good enough, but watching this miracle unfold before my eyes, I knew I was destined to do God's work through the power of the one true King. I simply had to trust and obey.

Rachael has little recollection of the accident. She does remember having to get new IVs that caused her great pain and resulted in many tears. She recalls avoiding looking at the needle, and instead raising her eyes up to look at the whimsical posters of monkeys and gorillas we had placed on the ceiling. Thankfully, most of her memories are pleasant ones. My daughter remembers riding her Big Wheel up and down the hallways of the hospital when she was well enough, and the candy stripers who brought her games. She recalls the big "Welcome Home" party we threw for her, and all the relatives and friends who shared in our celebration. She still smiles when she talks about getting the much longed-for gift of a Snoopy Sno-cone maker. It sits in her kitchen now.

Today, Rachael sees the events of her conception and birth as a redemption story. God took what could have been a dark mess and He created beautiful light from it.

Pat and I stayed together, weathering our storms, and are so happy we did. The Lord showed us how great His faithfulness is, and that He remains in the miracle business. We continue to cling to His promises, for He alone is worthy of our praise and our lives. We know that because of Rachael's miracle, but also because of the ones yet to come, God wasn't finished showing us His power.

HAVE YOU CONSIDERED . . .

- *Has there been a time in your life when there was nothing more you could do, but pray?*

- *Have you ever felt suffering was a direct result of your sin? Read Ephesians 1:7. "In Him we have redemption through His blood, the forgiveness of sins, in accordance with the riches of God's grace." How does this verse about the nature of God speak to you?*

- *Jesus performed many miracles during His life on earth. Do you believe He still does today?*

CHAPTER TWELVE

SETTING ANCHOR

1984

Although we were moving back to a familiar city, we were very different people than when we first left. We enrolled Rachael in kindergarten in our neighborhood school which was within walking distance. Even though the school was for Rachael, I was more excited than she about the fresh starts that awaited us: friendships, growth, memories, special events, and community.

I enthusiastically joined the Girl Scouts of the USA (GSUSA) and became a leader, serving in Rachael's Brownie troop. When I had envisioned being a mom, part of my dreams included participating in the Girl Scouts with my daughters. My own mother was good to get us to meetings, but I'd wished for her involvement. Little did I know how this volunteer activity was about to impact the rest of my life.

Pat took a new position in sales with a large company, Honeywell, working in the energy conservation field. Finding a job with a Fortune 100 company was a greater gift from God than we could have imagined. Following his initial interview, knowing hundreds of qualified candidates were under consideration for the position, concerned Pat. His prior sales experience came only from small industrial-scale companies, so he felt less than qualified. But divine guidance and his confidence won them over. This new position proved to be a life-changer for us. We felt the Lord was giving us a new chance to financially provide for our young family.

I continued to be a stay-at-home mom when we moved to Cincinnati while Pat began his new career. My decision to "just be a mom" shocked many people, as friends and relatives spoke similar concerns. "You are destined for greatness. I hate to see you wasting your life."

There were times I couldn't disagree with them. During my years in high school and college, I watched the Equal Rights Amendment tossed about in the legislature. It was not unusual to witness women's marches on television or to hear about the latest victory of a woman assuming a man's role and thus "breaking the glass ceiling." Women's rights were at the forefront of current events, and I was not fitting the new expectation.

For so long, I thought I'd be a lawyer. I even thought about running for a political office, since politics had always interested me. Instead of pursuing those goals, now I was staying at home.

Despite societal pressures at the time, I loved being with my kids and had a ball as their mom. Serving at their school, in our church, and in their Girl Scout troops gave me great joy. I busied myself in various activities and grew proud of my ability to juggle a lot of tasks at one time.

Before we even picked a house, Pat decided on our church during one of his relocation trips. We began attending Springdale Church of the Nazarene, where Pat and I continued maturing in our spiritual walk with God. Our discernment sharpened as our biblical worldview was heightened through personal Bible studies, in-depth conversations with other truth-seekers, and the knowledge we received from spiritual leaders. We began to notice secular humanism invading our kid's curriculum and media. What had been okay for us as high schoolers in the Seventies was no longer acceptable to us as parents. Now, we understood the consequences better.

> Our discernment sharpened as our biblical worldview was heightened through personal Bible studies, in-depth conversations with other truth-seekers, and the knowledge we received from spiritual leaders.

Pat and I loved all types of music, but our preferred genre was rock. When we wanted to relax on Friday nights, we played our vinyl. As we became more attuned to what we were listening to, certain lyrics made us pause and look at one another—usually at the same time. "Did you hear what that said?" we'd ask. Little by little, the Lord honed our ears, and we began to realize the potential negative effect many lyrics had on the mind of the listener. Soon, we couldn't keep our discoveries to ourselves.

Pat started working with one of our friends from church to develop an educational program for parents, and I gave my input as well. The intent was to raise awareness about the messages in the lyrics of music. Together we started conducting parenting classes, ignoring the fact that we had little to no authority, except for the moral barometer that convicted us to take action. Many attendees thanked us for opening their eyes. They didn't seem to care that we were not much older than their teenagers.

Our volunteer activities began to grow—at school, sports, scouts, and church. Then, I was asked to become the children's pastor. Although it was a volunteer position, I recognized its importance. I felt called to lobby for the children in the church, making an effort to pay attention to them and to begin investing in their guidance. At that time, kids' ministry was just a glorified babysitting service with poor curriculum and boring activities. I knew that if the church did not invest in their youngest members, it would most certainly lose them as they became teens. So, with deep passion, I continued to volunteer and pioneer for the children despite the long hours and no pay. I wanted to make sure every child had an opportunity to hear about our amazing Lord through refreshing and engaging curriculum.

This God-given burden to follow the biblical directive to "start children off on the way they should go, and even when they are old they will not turn from it" (Proverbs 22:6), became my life's mission. I had no idea my future would include battling a once venerable institution because of the importance of this message. I never dreamed I'd end up where I did—or that I'd find the courage to get there.

HAVE YOU CONSIDERED . . .

- *Is there a limit to the roles a woman can assume? Have you ever felt "less than" in your chosen role?*

- *The Lord never gives us a burden by mistake. In what areas do you have a fire in your belly to serve?*

- *Has there been a time in your life when you felt called to do something, but you didn't feel qualified? Consider 2 Corinthians 3:5 "Not that we are sufficient in ourselves to claim anything as coming from us, but our sufficiency is from God."*

CHAPTER THIRTEEN

AMERICAN HERITAGE

1985–1993

By 1985, my dad had suffered from MS for over twenty years when the family decided he needed more assistance than my mom and private in-home care nurses could provide. This difficult choice was hard on everyone. However, we were blessed to find a care facility that was not an old folks' home, but rather served middle-aged people with neurological disorders. The residents ranged from victims of cerebral palsy, stroke, car accidents, and like my father, those with MS.

The year 1985 also brought a bright spot—our third daughter, Katy, was born. I adored her beautiful blonde curls and bright green eyes, but she had severe colic and I thought for certain she would be our last child. Between raising three young children, managing Pat's growing career, my volunteer responsibilities, and visiting my dad, Pat and I had our hands full.

Understandably, once Dad went into the nursing facility, my mom began to focus more on herself and her own needs. Although Mom visited Dad regularly and tended to his physical health, she began a long-term relationship with another man. I coped with this as I did with other heartbreaking situations—I buried myself with life and a full calendar of activities.

Then, my prediction that Katy would be our last child was soon debunked. In 1988, our little guy, Jonathon, was born. Honestly, I was beginning to wonder how many kids it would take before we produced one who could carry on the Garibay family name, so we were delighted.

From the time he was born, our girls always called Jonathon "golden boy," because his arrival necessitated a larger car and a larger home. This time was especially memorable as it was in this neighborhood that I met Laurie Cullen, who became my life-long friend. We served together in many volunteer roles.

Much to my surprise, after years of patiently waiting, the church agreed to budget for a full-time children's ministry pastor. This was such great news and an answer to my prayers. I was asked to serve on the search committee to select the new leader for that position.

After months of interviewing other candidates but not finding one that was the right fit, the church offered me the position. I wanted to accept it quickly but slowed down to discuss it with Pat. I also needed to commit myself and the opportunity for prayer.

Soon after the church board offered me the role, Pat announced that he also had his own new opportunity, one that would mean a significant promotion. His sales performance was stellar, and he had demonstrated great aptitude in leadership and management. My husband had earned this advancement. Then he shared the rest of the news—the job was in McLean, Virginia, right outside of Washington, D.C., the murder capital of the world.

My heart sank. While I was ecstatic for Pat and his promotion, I was disappointed. This meant I could not accept the position I had long desired.

Once again, life took us away to another city. I felt guilty about leaving Dad again. It was 1990, and my father had been in the home for five years. But a promotion that presented itself through a company like Honeywell gave Pat no choice but to take it. This seemed to be the next right step for our family. We prayed and asked the Lord to close the doors of this move if it was not His will. Those doors never closed, and we packed up our home once again, sold the house, and headed to Virginia. The move was hard for Rachael, who was a tween at the time. She so loved her school, her Girl Scout troop, and had made good friends in Cincinnati.

> Through our experiential study of history during those days, we became acutely aware of the Judeo-Christian values upon which our country was founded. We could see the manifest destiny that was divinely appointed to our Nation's founders.

We loved our time in Virginia, it was a time of growing closer together as a couple and a family. We became immersed in the rich history of our American heritage. Most every weekend, one found the Garibay family at a historic site in the area. Those days with our young family were reminiscent of my happier childhood living in Boston. Our favorite landmark was the Lincoln Memorial, particularly the rarely-visited basement of the Memorial, which chronicled Lincoln's life of service to his country. Through our experiential study of history during those days, we became acutely aware of the Judeo-Christian values upon which our country was founded. We could see the manifest destiny that was divinely appointed to our Nation's founders.

In northern Virginia, I once again served the Girl Scouts by leading three troops. I also volunteered for the PTA and became the vice president. These outlets were a great way for us to build relationships with other families in the community.

All the while, we continued our spiritual growth through church attendance, enhanced by listening to daily radio shows that taught us more about a biblical worldview in modern society. We began to take note of the progressive nature of the public schools our children attended, and their curriculum designed to indoctrinate students in secular humanism. I became a watchdog, observing more activities and viewpoints that seemed questionable. The system certainly blurred the lens of our biblical worldview.

Our stay in Virginia was short-lived and after only three years, Honeywell presented yet another job opportunity for Pat. This one moved us back to Cincinnati. Although we loved our time in Virginia and the lessons learned there, we missed our families in Ohio. In 1993, we sold our home, packed up our possessions, and once again uprooted our family. We moved to West Chester, Ohio, which later became the birthplace of our life's purpose. We had no idea how God planned to use us in our home state . . . and far beyond.

HAVE YOU CONSIDERED . . .

• *Have you ever had a disabled relative who needed around-the-clock care that you could not provide? What, if anything, about that situation caused guilt in your heart?*

- *Have you ever had to forfeit a dream for another's benefit?*

- *Can you look back on a time in your life and see why God placed you where He did when He did? How did He use that experience in your future?*

CHAPTER FOURTEEN

THE TRUTH

1993

After all of our moves, I must say I was very sick of relocation. Upon our return to Ohio, Pat and I were both excited and hopeful that we would not need to pull up stakes again.

We anticipated that our new home would house our children through their college years while providing space for their friends. It had ample room for visits from our extended families and neighbors. We once more became very involved in the community, schools, sports, and scouts, and returned to our beloved church. But, despite the familiarity of our church and environment, The Lord was about to interrupt the comfortable life we were building.

As Pat and I lay in bed watching the evening news one night, the anchor's report made me sit up straight. I could not believe what I was hearing. Girl Scouts USA was proposing a change to its foundational principle.

Since its inception, serving God had been at the heart of their program. But that year at their national convention, they were going to vote to place an asterisk next to the word "God," allowing "flexibility" in its use in the Promise that each girl recites at every meeting.

I was a leader for each of my three girl's troops, a troop organizer for West Chester, Ohio, and an area delegate. You might say I was super involved in Girl Scouting in my local council. Yet, I wondered, *how could this new foundational philosophy to Girl Scouts USA be happening without my or other volunteers' prior knowledge?*

Pat was sitting next to me and, with his eyes fixed on the TV, gave me an elbow nudge. He said, "What are you going to do about that?" as he pointed at the screen and then looked at me. I could feel anxiety begin to rise in my chest. What was I going to do about it?

Awake most of the night, I watched the dawn slowly unfold. My thoughts tormented me, and questions flooded my mind. *Why would the convention delegates be so dismissive about the role of God in Girl Scouting by putting an asterisk by His name? What would prompt such a change from the origins of the organization?*

To me, it seemed like this apparent diminishing role of God was the reason for all of the moral relativism (lack of universal or absolute set of moral principles) that I had begun seeing in my daughter's handbooks and in the *Leader* magazine. The new programs were also concerning. *What was really going on here?* I wondered. It seemed an enemy was underfoot, quietly confusing our troops and destroying the camp.

I needed to process the thoughts swirling in my mind about the Girl Scouts. I had seen the nuances of a mission shift in Girl Scouting through their materials and recent trainings but changing "God" in the Girl Scout Promise was just too much. I wondered if I was being too sensitive, exacerbating an issue, perhaps making a mountain out of an ant hill. I needed to talk to others to see if they shared my concerns. So, I invited a few friends over to my house later that week to talk about this impending change.

I opened the conversation. "How do you feel about the Girl Scouts decision to diminish God at the convention?"

Immediately, the women expressed confusion and outrage. "What are they thinking?"

"Why would they do that?"

"How can they make this kind of change without talking to their volunteers?"

We all agreed our girls were under attack, not only at the hands of the Girl Scouts, but also from society in general. The Girl Scouts were not the only ones beginning to teach moral relativism in youth organizations across the nation.

Juliette Gordon Low, the founder of the Girl Scouts, clearly instilled biblical values in the organization at its conception. I loved collecting historic Girl Scout books and learned that Juliette regularly read the Bible, believed in God, and created the organization to provide a clear sense of right and wrong. She wanted God's truth to be central and acknowledgement of Him to be foundational. Moving away from alignment with Juliette's vision, the Girl Scouts were heading down a path dangerously different than its foundress's vision.

Over the years, minor tweaks to the Promise had taken place. However, none of the changes were as dramatic as this change. Placing an asterisk by God's name, thus allowing members to insert whatever god they believed in or no word at all if they were atheist, essentially diminished the role of God in Girl Scouting.

My friends and I had a heart for girls—we were raising our own while voluntarily working with others. We knew that if we could look inside these girls' hearts and minds, we'd find a lot of anxiety and body image concerns along with a deep lack of self-worth, and the list of issues continued. We counted on the Girl Scouts' wholesome program to serve as an antidote to the societal ills we were seeing. But without God in the program, how could there be a solid foundation for these future women?

That night, as we sat around the table in my kitchen, my friends and I decided we could not sit back—we needed to take action. We agreed to pray about what that action would be and to share what we were learning with others, inviting them to join us in finding a solution.

We had no idea how many difficulties we would face in order to take on this giant, the Girl Scouts of the USA. We often felt like Don Quixote, in *Man of La Mancha,* battling windmills. We questioned our sanity and certainly did not know if we had what it took to fight, plan, and organize.

The Girl Scouts had remained a time-honored, venerable institution for so long. I believed they were worth saving. They had certainly helped me as a girl. I wanted them to see the Pandora's box they were opening with their decisions. I was willing to try. I had to try!

Through my years as a Girl Scout troop leader, I met many girls who reminded me of my younger self. I even met a girl whose dad had multiple sclerosis. The girls who came to our meetings came from a variety of family situations, not all of them ideal.

When I got involved, I hoped to provide memorable, positive, and influential opportunities during their girlhood. I used Girl Scouting as a type of ministry that allowed the girls to see my love for God and the importance of being confident as a result of our identity in Him. Girl Scouts and their

> I thought if I could help one girl escape a difficult childhood for even an hour a week, or for several hours during a weekend campout, my time and heart investment would be well spent.

methods had seemed the perfect canvas for realizing this dream. I thought if I could help one girl escape a difficult childhood for even an hour a week, or for several hours during a weekend campout, my time and heart investment would be well spent.

My friends and I vowed to continue the discussion and attempt to make the necessary changes to keep our girls innocent and godly. As I said goodbye to the last of the ladies that evening, I knew my future was about to change. As uncomfortable as it was, the need was obvious—we had to dig deeper into the issues of the Girl Scouts.

Quite frankly, it would have been easier to shrug off the concerns in hopes that someone else would pick up the mantle of leadership. But I couldn't ignore what I saw, and I couldn't wait for someone else. I believed that my husband and me, as well as our small band of friends, were called to take a stand for such a time as this (Esther 4:13-14). We were counting on the truth of God's nature—that He does not call the equipped, but He equips the called.

Soon, God began igniting a fire in my mind and heart. His light allowed my eyes to gain a clear, discerning focus regarding what was happening within the ranks of the Girl Scouts. With each meeting, my rag-tag group of parents and I uncovered more controversial issues. During this time, I was reminded of what Joshua said when he spoke to the children of

Israel, "But as for me and my house, we will serve the LORD" (Joshua 24:15).

Silence was not an option for me. It was time to work toward change.

HAVE YOU CONSIDERED . . .

- *Have you ever been confronted with a truth that you did not want to believe?*

- *When the truth was verified, were you initially dismissive of the need for you to take action?*

- *When thinking of character development programs, how important is absolute truth?*

- *When society becomes more diverse, is God still the authority?*

CHAPTER FIFTEEN

SOLID FOUNDATION

1994

I was frazzled, exhausted, and ready to lose my mind.

Pat was busy adjusting to his new role, including much travel. He also decided to go to graduate school to get his MBA. I was doing all I could to make the transfer from Virginia to Cincinnati go well for our kids, ages six to fifteen. My children went to four different schools and were involved in sports, scouts, and church. To add to the mayhem, we had a mutt who ran out the door every time it opened and with four kids and their friends, the door was opened a lot. We spent many evenings canvassing the neighborhood, looking for that dog.

More and more parents attended our weekly kitchen-table meetings, and our investigations revealed the apparent agenda of the Girl Scouts. It was clear that our little group was making a difference and it was time to create an official entity. This team was formed purely out of the cry of so many concerned parents' hearts, and for that reason, we named the group C.R.Y. We were now Caring Responsibly for our Youth.

The concerns of C.R.Y. were quickly shared across the country. Women from different areas of the nation began to call and mail letters of concern to our post office box. Their correspondence told of personal experiences and discoveries. Suddenly, C.R.Y. had ambassadors who were united in exposing the truth of the Girl Scouts. Together, we uncovered many distasteful programs and inappropriate retreats, which validated our crusade and the need to shine a light on these issues.

A shared concern about the role of God in Girl Scouting was the primary driver for all involved. An increasing lack of moral truth crept into every area of the organization, even the girls' handbooks. According to the 1993 edition of the *Brownie Girl Scout Handbook,* "There is no 'right' way to live, look, talk, dress, eat, or act."

Another source stated, "A Girl Scout meeting is not the place for prayers and hymns." As a matter of fact, my own Girl Scout troop was warned not to sing Christmas carols in a community Christmas parade. It seemed to me that not only was God becoming optional in the Girl Scout Promise, but He was being kicked out of the program entirely.

Another issue with which parents were concerned was the inappropriate way the local Girl Scout council treated the subject of sex education. The curriculum used was information-based, but devoid of morality and values. I first heard about this approach on the *Focus on the Family* news program. I was shocked to hear my hometown's council mentioned in that broadcast, along with its controversial "sex camp." Soon, my thirteen-year-old daughter received an invitational brochure in the mail, titled *Sexuality and You Weekend Retreat.* This was the very program I had just heard about on the radio. Although the brochure appeared innocuous, I knew the Girl Scouts would not be treating the topic in a holistic manner. I wondered how many parents might send their daughters, not understanding the dangers and depths of the teaching.

Finally, there was the issue of the GSUSA's hiring practice of allowing homosexual volunteers and staff. In one instance, a Girl Scout staffer in Michigan was asked to recruit homeschooled girls to attend summer camp. But she felt compelled to alert parents of her local council's hiring practice regarding homosexuality, so she was fired.

Because C.R.Y. was taking a stand, we were also getting a lot of objections from people, and sadly, we lost many friendships. Some called us "CRY-babies" and made jest of our concerns. It clearly felt like a time of abandonment and sacrifice. I took comfort in the words of A. W. Tozer, who said, "The man after God's own heart must be dead to the opinion of his friends as well as his enemies." Many of our friends didn't have eyes to see or ears to hear the message at that time—or the foresight to envision the battle that needed to be fought. Today, we are dealing with things unimagined back then.

> I took comfort in the words of A. W. Tozer, who said, "The man after God's own heart must be dead to the opinion of his friends as well as his enemies."

More recently, there has been yet another change in the ever-evolving GSUSA. While the Girl Scouts has now removed the asterisk by the Lord's name on its national website (some local councils have kept the asterisk), they still allow girls to define God in whatever way they believe. The frenzy that resulted from this change tainted the name of Girl Scouts in many minds. They now "hide" their true agenda around the role of God in Girl Scouting—only upon further investigation can parents discover this.

Parents have a God-given responsibility to fully know what their children are being taught. They should not have to go through smoke and mirrors to discover it—particularly from a once-venerable character-building institution trusted for generations. But truth is the only way to freedom. And sometimes, there are dark things people try to hide. However, God always sees.

HAVE YOU CONSIDERED . . .

• *Have you ever lost relationships due to your moral convictions?*

• *Does God's Word support the philosophy of moral relativism? Consider Colossians 2:8 which says, "See to it that no one takes you captive through hollow and deceptive philosophy, which depends on human tradition and the elemental spiritual forces of this world rather than on Christ."*

CHAPTER SIXTEEN

DESTRUCTIVE DISCOVERIES

1994

As I mentioned before, part of my concerns with the new Girl Scouts became apparent as Rachael, who was in my cadette troop, received that invitation to a Girl Scout retreat. It was the first time we ever recalled her receiving mail from the Girl Scouts addressed directly to her. According to the pamphlet *Sexuality and You Weekend Retreat,* the event was to "help increase their knowledge, enhance their self-esteem, and help them identify their own values in the area of sexuality."[2]

At a troop pool party, parents of girls in my troop asked me what I knew about this retreat. Again, a check in my gut told me not to blindly trust the Girl Scouts with this important topic. I shared with the parents that I recently felt great misgivings about the direction of the Girl Scouts. I assured them I would see what I could find out about this "retreat."

_____

2 *Sexuality and You* pamphlet, Great Rivers Girl Scout Council, 1993

C.R.Y.'s mission to investigate was needed. Several parents wanted to know more, and they needed to know the truth. After all, these were their precious daughters.

A local pastor heard about our C.R.Y. group. He invited us to share our concerns with a local Christian radio station by broadcasting a series of segments on his show, *At the Crossroads*. We named these shows "Awareness Campaigns." During the broadcasts, we asked the audience for testimonials of parents whose daughters had attended the retreat of which my daughter was invited. Since the local council had been conducting this retreat since 1983, we thought some parents had certainly sent their daughters.

The C.R.Y. parents believed the seemingly harmless brochure sent to Girl Scouts across Cincinnati probably did not reveal the true depth of topics and activities shared during the weekend. Going on the radio with our plea would allow us an opportunity to learn more and open the eyes of other parents.

We continued to broadcast the radio show week after week with the pastor. A handful of moms spoke on the radio show, but no one called in to share their experience with that retreat. Then one day, the show's producer received a call. It came from the executive director of our local council. She wanted to find out who was speaking out, and she agreed to a meeting with the "whistleblowers." Still believing I could make a positive change in Girl Scouts, I thought this meeting might prove productive.

The pastor said if we met with the director, we should request she bring the *Sexuality and You* facilitator's guide. Surprisingly, the council director agreed.

I was nervous about the meeting. At the time, I was a stay-at-home mom with big insecurity issues. I just wanted to be a mom, not a superhero. I prayed, asking the Holy Spirit to give me strength and wisdom, because I knew I could not do this on my own.

The nerve-inducing day arrived. My new friend drove down from Michigan to be at my side during the meeting with the executive director and a board member from the council. They were polished businesspeople and we were just Christ followers.

On the evening of the meeting, I parked my minivan outside of the church at the scheduled time. I took in a deep breath and my heart throbbed quickly in my chest. I bowed my head praying out loud before getting out of my vehicle. "Holy Spirit. I need help. I don't know what I'm going to say or how I should act. These people are pros, and you're sending me in there to meet with them. While I would never ask to do this sort of thing, Lord, let this not be my will but yours. Give me the words to say and the humility in my heart to be kind and loving and a true reflection of You." I lifted my bowed head, took in another deep breath, and looked through the front window, wondering if the attendees had already assembled. Then, I got out of the van.

My positive attitude hoped this discussion would lead to a change in the Girl Scouts, but it was clear throughout the meeting that my optimism would not be fulfilled. Despite the tense atmosphere and the

> I trusted God and knew He would take care of the outcome.

anxiety that probably took years off my life, I did receive the one thing I was after: the *Sexuality and You* facilitator's guide. I left the meeting feeling somewhat discouraged, yet I was buoyed because I had been obedient. I trusted God and knew He would take care of the outcome.

I returned home, exhausted and emotionally spent. I finished my evening as any caring mother would—by perusing the facilitator's guide cover to cover. Those two hours of reading were interrupted by my sobbing and mental tirades. *How dare they? What gives them the right? And they say their mission is to raise caring, competent, and confident girls?* I was disgusted, disheartened, and despondent.

You might wonder why I was so emotional. My own lack of biblical understanding surrounding sexuality had haunted me into my young adult years, and I wanted to save others the painful consequences I endured. From experience, I knew this topic was one that needed to be treated with the respect it deserved, to protect young women and men, and this curriculum was far from that. Some highlights from the facilitator's guide deemed appropriate for twelve and thirteen-year-old girls included the following:

Starting on a Friday night at a Girl Scout Camp, the retreat was to kick off with songs and games in an effort for the girls to meet one another. The attendees would then be told to prepare for bed and snuggle into their sleeping bags. The facilitator was instructed to read in a "grandmotherly manner" Lois Gould's *X: A Fabulous Child's Story*.[3]

This story was originally published in 1972 in *Ms. Magazine,* during the height of the women's rights movement. The maga-

---

3 Teacher's Manual—Human Sexuality Retreat for Cadette Girl Scouts, Marianne S. McGrath M.D., Great Rivers Girl Scout Council Inc., Pg. 18-25, 54, 41, 50, 68

zine's cofounder was abortion advocate Gloria Steinem, commonly referred to as the founding mother of feminism.

The intent of reading the story at bedtime was to lull the girls asleep with the notion of not having a gender assigned to them, like Baby X. This would allow them to transcend stereotypes and find true success in the world.

The next morning would begin with a "getting-to-know-you game." According to the guide, "There is a desire to introduce and define a number of terms that relate to a variety of sexual expressions." The guide continues by defining a variety of sexual terms during a game known as "Who Am I?" Leaders were told to laminate flash cards with specific terms and have presenters affix a card to each girl's back with masking tape. The terms include, but are not limited to:

- dyke
- voyeur
- fetish
- sadist
- masochist
- whore
- hooker
- transvestite
- zoophilic
- nymphomania

The girls are encouraged to share with one another what they know about each term. Again, this is considered twelve and thirteen-year-old appropriate by the Great Rivers Girl Scout Council.

The facilitators are then asked to provide sufficient embellishment and clarification to the girls' discussion to make the following points:

- There is a spectrum of sexual feelings and expressions, and most people fall in the middle of a bell-shaped distribution rather than at either extreme.

• Individuals may move in any direction along the continuum of expressions during the course of a lifetime.

The guide added one particular point. It is extremely important to present material in a nonjudgmental fashion

After the twelve- and thirteen-year-old girls spent the weekend listening to the bedtime story of Baby X, viewing a vaginal vault with a flashlight, touching a replica of male genitalia, discussing various forms of contraception and playing the "Who Am I?" guessing game, the parents would arrive. But there was an additional warning.

The facilitator was to caution the girls that their "parents may have a bias around sexuality and may have experienced a conspiracy of silence about sexuality which will require (them) courage to confront."

After reading this at the time, I felt the curriculum provided a calculated plan to indoctrinate girls, and today, I believe the results of the curriculum are evident. For me, the Girl Scouts' strategy clearly intended to take away the innocence of children and usurp the parents' rights to moral guidance around the topic of sexuality. It subtly undermined a parent's authority, and encouraged girls to disrespect their parents' moral guidance.

I was troubled for days after reading that material. I imagined how confused the girls who attended the retreat must have felt upon returning home. *How could the parents of these attendees undo the damage that had been done to their precious daughters?*

I needed a break from the heaviness of the subject, but that was not going to happen. One of the original parents of C.R.Y., Laurie, along with Pat and I, were asked to be interviewed by a local TV station, WCPO. When the interview aired, we were given a wide audience with whom to share our concerns about the non-value-based program for Girl Scouts. The fact that twenty-six local volunteers had left the Girl Scouts because they shared our concerns supported our message.

A Girl Scout mom and avid talk radio listener named Carolyn called into the show. "I'm a Brownie leader and I recently read an article called, 'The Cookie Crumbles,'" Carolyn said. "It made me aware of how much the Girls Scouts are changing. I've talked with several other leaders, and we all share your concerns."

After a brief exchange on live radio, we gave her our office number, which at the time was really Laurie's second house phone line. Carolyn left a message immediately, and I called her back the next day.

We spoke for over an hour, realizing how closely our hearts were aligned. Neither of us fully realized the part Carolyn would play in our movement going forward.

In 1994, many members of C.R.Y. were beginning to notice the strong advocacy of the lesbian lifestyle in the Girl Scouts. Some local councils were promoting a book entitled, *On My Honor: Lesbians Reflect on their Scouting Experience*. In it, author Nancy Manahan discusses the involvement of lesbians in Girl Scouts, including her bold statement that one in three Girl Scout administrators identifies as lesbian. Carolyn, a former journalist, began investigating.

On internet bulletin boards, Carolyn posted a note that read, *I'm curious to see if your council allows lesbians to serve on staff and as volunteers.* We were shocked to see several people respond affirmatively, from all over the country. Locally, our own council sponsored an ad in an alternative lifestyle newspaper seeking volunteers. The extent of infiltration astounded those of us who did not want our daughters exposed to teachings that went against every fiber of our faith.

Girl Scout leaders with a biblical worldview were leaving the GSUSA in mass exodus because of the changes. Many women who had enjoyed the Scouts organization and its original traditions in their own girlhoods could no longer ignore the subtle, yet drastic shift. Still others allowed their appreciation for the long tradition of Girl Scouting to trump the truth they were seeing and tried to continue with the Girl Scouts' organization, at least for a while. Of course, we were not yet aware that the insidious takeover of Girls Scouts was already this deep, on the radio show that introduced us to Carolyn.

Afterward, WCPO then interviewed the executive director of the council. But the story of our local sex camp went far beyond the Cincinnati city limits. It hit the *Cleveland Plain Dealer,* the *Washington Times,* and eventually the nationally syndicated *G. Gordon Liddy Show,* whose feature story led to the closing of the retreat.

After running this Girl Scout program for over a decade, the council claimed that the event had been closed because of "bad publicity," without ever apologizing for having used material inappropriate for young girls. It seemed the Girl Scouts' agenda for sex education and desensitizing our youth was more important for the organization than some momentary bad publicity.

In my opinion, even today, the GSUSA continues to venture into the murky waters of sex education, progressive politics, and promotion of feminist leaders. Secular worldviews envelope this program, leaving the member to base their character development on the morals, or lack thereof, of today's society. How difficult for today's girl to navigate her world without a firm foundation of right and wrong. It's important to understand the truth behind schemes.

HAVE YOU CONSIDERED . . .

- *Have you ever chosen a program for your child based on surface values which you later regretted?*

- *Why is it so important to protect the innocence of children?*

- *Why is it vital for parents to teach a biblical worldview to their children in regard to the topic of human sexuality?*

- *How have you dealt with the ramifications of a poor choice you made in regard to your child's exposure to inappropriate topics?*

CHAPTER SEVENTEEN

BETRAYAL

1994

After the exposure and forced closing of our local sex camp, C.R.Y. was determined to shine a light on the apparently methodical forfeiture of the innocence of girls. During this time of spiritual warfare, it seemed new discoveries were constant, and the days were filled with a heavy, dark feeling that comes only from the adversary of humanity, Satan. After much prayer and many meetings, C.R.Y. continued to counter the concerns we had with action.

We had believed in the rich tradition of Girl Scouting, and as parents we believed that the antidote to the ills of the GSUSA would be to reveal its agenda through a public awareness campaign. I continued to hope that public pressure would change the schemes of those few in the leadership of the GSUSA.

C.R.Y. appealed to national delegates at the Minneapolis national convention to reconsider the adoption of Proposal 3, which allowed flexibility in the wording of spiritual beliefs in the Girl Scout Promise. We did this in every way imaginable—via fax, door-to-door petitions, hand-delivered telegrams, and phone calls. We held informational sessions around the city entitled, *Keeping the Traditions of Girl Scouting.* In addition, we wanted to nominate a sensible Christian for the board of directors of the local council, hoping to persuade the leadership of the errors in its ways.

Even through all of this, my heart's desire was still to see the Girl Scouts of the USA make a positive change. I wanted us to all go back to being the happy Girl Scouts we had once been. I felt we had one more chance to try to make a difference.

In March 1994, it was determined that C.R.Y. would provide a candidate for the council's board of directors. This candidate was my husband, Pat, an accomplished businessman and community volunteer. The council had mandated that in the case of a candidate offered from the floor, their biographies must be submitted to the council two weeks prior to the annual meeting. This time was to allow the council to thoroughly investigate candidates that were not on their pre-selected slate.

I was a nervous wreck again, anticipating all the possible outcomes that could come from this annual meeting and Pat's candidacy. Finally, the day arrived.

Our small group walked into the large auditorium filled with people. While I engaged with many familiar faces when I entered, I knew our group was unwelcomed. We carefully picked a spot where Pat could easily walk up to speak, if given the opportunity. I was thankful that at least the chairs were comfortable, even though I felt the agonizing pangs of anxiety.

I kept my head down while I read some of the material we were hoping to present. As I looked up, I noticed a woman sitting directly in front of me. She wore a pentagram ring. The insignia reminded me this was not a battle between people, but rather of the spiritual realm. My breath caught, and my lips lifted a prayer of protection.

My stomach was in knots, and the surroundings felt surreal. The suspicion in the room was palpable. Every word seemed measured and manipulated. The typical agenda of an annual meeting was followed to a "t" and moved ever so slowly. Oddly, in this session, a break was suddenly called by the parliamentarian, and frenzied activity ensued.

During the recess, two microphones in stands were placed in the aisles of the auditorium. Lines of people began to gather behind each stand. It appeared that the council had identified a couple of people to serve as plants in the audience. Without warning or proper announcement, these people began spewing false allegations against Pat specifically and C.R.Y. in general. It was manipulated mayhem.

After the "volunteers" had their say, the meeting was officially called back to order. The vote on the slate for the council's board of directors, plus Pat, was taken and tallied. The results were announced by a board member who claimed that C.R.Y.'s candidate received zero votes. We heard gasps throughout the auditorium. Dozens of people in the audience mentioned to C.R.Y. members that they had voted for Pat, and I know I certainly did.

Then unbelievably, a motion was made to destroy the ballots, and the board members approved it. We knew there was no recourse, no recount, and for us, no hope.

That night, I knew my time with the Girl Scouts had ended. My thirteen years as a volunteer and my five years as a girl member had taken up a good portion of my life. Pat and I returned home that evening to our waiting kids who were all awake, even though it was past their bedtimes.

I angrily proclaimed, "I will NEVER represent or promote Girl Scouts ever again—never!" I don't believe my children ever saw me so angry and upset. I removed my beloved Girl

Scout pin tab and hurled it across the room—and I never looked back.

Afterward, the words of Habakkuk resounded in my heart:

"How long, O Lord, must I call for help?
But you do not listen!
'Violence is everywhere!' I cry,
but you do not come to save.
Must I forever see these evil deeds?
Why must I watch all this misery?"
Habakkuk 1:2-3

Much like Habakkuk, I felt defeated and hopeless. My faith would be tested. How could I even think of starting a new organization? But never discount the power of God.

HAVE YOU CONSIDERED . . .

- *What do you do when you experience disappointment from a once trusted source?*

- *How do we recognize when we are in the midst of spiritual warfare? What serves as your armor? Ephesians 6:11 tells us to, "Put on the full armor of God so you can take your stand against the devil's schemes."*

I removed my beloved Girl Scout pin tab and hurled it across the room—and I never looked back.

CHAPTER EIGHTEEN

START SOMETHING NEW

1995

I needed wisdom and comfort, and Dad always provided that for me. I simply wanted to be with him and went to visit after that horrible Girl Scout annual meeting.

Even from his prostrate position in his bed, he could tell I was down. "So, tell me about the most recent escapades of the Girl Scouts," he grinned.

I was usually his sunshine girl, always ready with a smile and a bubbly laugh. But not today. I shared what happened to Pat during the board member vote for the Girl Scouts. I'll never forget what he said.

"Patti, why curse the darkness when you can light a candle? Start something new."

Dad's advice immediately moved me to tears. I knew he would have hugged me at that moment, if he could. But he'd done more than that. With this simple yet wise statement, my earthly father encouraged me to follow the plan of my heavenly Father. Dad's wisdom sparked the flame for the creation of the American Heritage Girls.

My father's words will resonate in my heart for eternity, and they reminded me of God's encouragement in scripture.

> *"You are the light of the world. A city set on a hill cannot be hidden. Nor do people light a lamp and put it under a basket, but on a stand, and it gives light to all in the house. In the same way, let your light shine before others, so that they may see your good works and give glory to your father, who is in heaven"* (Matthew 5:14-16 NIV).

This scripture became the foundation of our organization.

Dad and I laughed and cried together that day. His inability to walk or lead a normal life gave my father every reason to be self-centered, yet he used his energy to encourage others. That was my dad, so loving and kind. He'd made it clear I had to continue the fight.

Despite having people supporting me in this venture, I felt alone, defeated, ineffective, and scared. Though this was the time I needed to trust God explicitly, I started questioning Him. I went back to the Word and opened up the book of Habakkuk again. Just as He did when fears threated to keep me from writing this book, God responded to my plea. I felt the Holy Spirit nudging me to do something besides curse the darkness.

> *Then the Lord replied: 'Write down the revelation and make it plain on tablets so that a herald may run with it. For the revelation awaits an appointed time; it speaks of the end and will not prove false. Though it lingers, wait for it; it will certainly come and will not delay. See, the enemy is puffed up; his desires are not upright— but the righteous person will live by his faithfulness,'* (Habakkuk 2:2-4).

The message was clear—the Lord had a plan and He wanted to use me as part of what He wanted to accomplish. How could this be?

I argued the case in my mind. *I am too busy, too unqualified, too needy, and totally too harried. I am not good at anything, including motherhood, wifedom, sainthood, or even being a daughter.* I felt like I was a jack-of-all-trades and a master of none.

> I'm exactly the type of person God calls to do His work on earth. He uses people just like me and—in case you are wondering—just like you! People who consider themselves less than, are people God sees as enough.

But then, I realized I'm exactly the type of person God calls to do His work on earth. He uses people just like me and—in case you are wondering—just like you! People who consider themselves less than are people God sees as enough.

The gears were in motion, and out of our small gathering of friends came the concept of a new group, a new program. We had no idea what we were doing or how to even form an alternative scouting program for our daughters. But, in the typical providence of God, He made a way for us to proceed.

My friend from Michigan suggested a name for our group. "What about American Heritage Girls?" she said.

I immediately loved the name.

For me, Pat and my parents' service in the military underscored the high cost of freedom and the importance of sharing this message with future generations. And more recently, my heart had been pricked by my study of American history and its Christian foundations. Apart from the monuments in Washington, D.C., where God's name is engraved, I barely recognized the U.S. as a nation founded on biblical values. The schools, youth organizations, political parties, and laws all seemed to point to secular humanism as the current belief system in America. I wondered, *what if this new organization could turn the tide and influence young women to carry the torch of their forefathers?*

The American Heritage Girls (AHG) formed in 1994. Following my dad's encouragement and with much prayer, I started to slowly walk out my call. The Lord was so patient with all of us, but super patient with me. At that time, I was not the Christian I am today. It took me a while to figure out that it was okay if I did not fit the typical "Christian mold" of the quiet, submissive, contemplative, feminine woman. I am an outspoken extrovert with strong opinions and a bias for action, not to mention my tendency for sarcasm. These traits were not evident in the Christian role models I had seen up to that point in my life. Therefore, I discounted my ability to lead a ministry and be used by the Lord. Surely, someone else was better suited for the task than me.

As a testament to how the Lord saw me and my abilities, crazy occurrences started happening that could have only come from Him. He started bringing all sorts of people across our paths.

For instance, a man read an article about our fledging group and contacted Laurie. She set up a time to meet, so Laurie and I went to his house in northern Kentucky. Remember, this was the Nineties, so when he began to talk about something called a website it was completely foreign to us.

The man said we would need such a site to unite people together across the nation and the world. At the time, I guess he believed in this organization more than we did.

As we walked out of his home, Laurie and I looked at each other, stumped. We said in unison, "What in the world was he talking about?" Then we burst out in laughter like a couple of schoolgirls. We filed the information away for the future in the far-fetched chance we would ever need it. I still wonder if God chuckled at our naiveté over His bigger plan.

I am always amazed at the way the Lord lights up our lives, when we let Him. Pat had finally completed his MBA program which focused a great deal on how to start a business. What he learned in that program was used immediately, not just for his job but also for this new organization we were attempting to launch. Over the years, I have learned there really are no coincidences, only God instances.

For me, it was critical to have a high level of girl input while building this program for them—from uniforms to badges to membership pins to field trips. We involved as many of our daughters and their friends as possible around the kitchen table and listened to their opinions.

We held our first AHG meeting on September 13, 1995. Most of the girls at that meeting came from the Girl Scout troop I'd led in the area. Our first troop was numbered 895, reflecting the month and year of AHG's incorporation in the state of Ohio.

I contacted Carolyn, the woman who had reached out through the radio interview we'd done and let her know about our complete departure from GSUSA. She and her co-leader enthusiastically got involved. Of the ten AHG troops in 1995, theirs was the only one started outside of West Chester. But this very humble beginning sparked a flame that still blazes today.

Our first full year as American Heritage Girls was tough, actually, I would say excruciating. Most of the founding parents from the kitchen table soon left, dealing with varying seasons of life and different priorities. We understood, but it still presented a hardship for us. These were friends who were there during the difficult time of sorting through the Girl Scout issues. The adrenaline-rich battle with the Girl Scouts was over, and it was time to do the even more difficult and focused work of building a new program.

Figuring out what worked, what needed improvement, and what needed to be cut required much time, talent, and financial resource. Birthing an organization is hard on the mind and soul. We continued with the few parents who could stay involved, and who today have made a difference that has impacted tens of thousands of families over the last twenty-five years.

The news of our new organization quickly spread, causing us to hurry up and create the foundations of the program. We identified program emphases, instituted a handful of badges, developed adult training, and designed spirit wear. At this time, the Lord also delivered the AHG Oath during one of my late-night writing sessions. To this day it remains unchanged:

I promise to love God,
Cherish my family,
Honor my country,
and serve in my community.

We really didn't expect any expansion, especially early on, so the interest from those outside of our small group surprised us. We knew we had to take the growth seriously. I learned about the necessary steps to becoming a legal entity. We formed a board, incorporated in the state of Ohio, and created our bylaws. Later that year, we received our 501(c)(3) designation of non-profit status from the Internal Revenue Service.

I was deemed director and president of AHG and received a whopping salary of one dollar. I sensed that God had planned so much more than I could possibly do, and I discovered early on that it would take a village to pull this off.

God brought many people to help us, which served as confirmation that this was not a work of human beings, but rather a work of the Lord. Trailblazing adults provided a variety of skills, but along with their own relationship with Jesus Christ, they also had a desire for girls to understand their identity in Him.

When I was young, I was a shy girl and hated to talk to older people—shoot, I even made my sister prank call when we both agreed to play jokes on others. I always chickened out. I carried this trait into my adulthood.

For AHG, I needed pro bono legal assistance. I found it through networking via a friend, Phil, who helped during the Girl Scout days. I had to swallow my fear to make that phone call.

After I hung up the phone, I trembled as I reported to Pat excitedly. "This legal firm is willing to prepare everything we need for our non-profit application. For free!" This was one of many miracles God performed during the early years.

AHG had many ups and downs when we began. I commonly refer to this time of our development as our "skinned knees" period. We forged ahead anyway, tripping and falling, picking ourselves up, and dusting ourselves off. Then, we'd fall on our battered knees, bloodied from the falls, and pray,

"Lord, what do You want us to do here? Why is this going the way it's going or NOT going the way it should?"

There were lots of tears, lots of head shaking, lots of disbelief. I wavered between total commitment and total guilt. My kids needed my attention, my husband needed my attention, and my dad needed my attention. But through it all, I suspected we were on the right track. I knew I was allowing the Holy Spirit to guide me—to guide us. So, I did my best to meet everyone else's needs, while I tended the American Heritage Girls' flame God had sparked.

My husband also struggled during these times. I would not have known, had he not been so willing to be transparent and vulnerable. His changes impacted the trajectory of our lives, and the future of AHG.

HAVE YOU CONSIDERED . . .

- *Do you really believe if God calls you to do something that He will provide the resources to do it with?*

- *Have you ever felt called to do something that seemed to be unnecessary, yet you did it anyway? Looking back, are you able to see how God used that insignificant instance for the bigger picture?*

- *How do "skinned knee" events present opportunities for learning and spiritual growth in your life?*

- *Do you get upset when friends and family abandon your cause? In Ephesians 4:1-6 it says, ". . . I urge you to live a life worthy of the calling you have received, be completely humble and gentle; be patient, bearing with one another in love. Make every effort to keep the unity of the Spirit through the bond of peace." What is Paul calling us to do in this verse?*

CHAPTER NINETEEN

BIBLICAL LEADERSHIP

The concept of marriage was created by the Lord Himself. The marriage between Himself and the church is the perfect representation of His desires for marriage between His people. My journey is not my journey—it is *our* journey.

Together Pat and I have labored, held one another up when we were down, and provided accountability when necessary. I have been blessed with a wise husband whose reflection and understanding of our commitment would prove helpful to any couple. I pray you will be blessed by his perspective of how he grew during the time of American Heritage Girls' start. Next, you will hear directly from Pat.

***

Do you remember the first time, maybe as a child, you initially became aware that there really is a God? I went to church every Sunday and attended a Catholic school from first grade through high school, so I regularly heard about Him. But the first encounter I recall truly engaging with the Creator was in grade school, when I heard a missionary talk about his work in Africa.

I was a naturalist at heart (starting at the tender age of six) and was always fascinated with nature, especially in Africa (I loved watching Tarzan). However, when I heard about how this missionary brought Jesus to a people who had never heard of our Savior, of our God, it touched me. I truly felt the presence of the Lord at that time and committed (in my mind) that I would do great things in Africa for Him. Besides, I could hang with the gorillas while serving in ministry. Such are the dreams of a ten-year-old.

The key word here is "I."

"I" did not yet understand that I was a sinful person, and that my life's work needed to be in submission to God's will. I was always a competitive individual, and being taller than my peers, I tended to succeed in sports. I was bored at school, getting A's without a lot of effort. This started me on a path of thinking I could do just about anything, if I put my mind to it.

Pride.

"I" could do anything if "I" put my mind to it. If you're good at something, there is nothing wrong with taking pride in your performance, right? Well, James 4:6 tells us:

"But he gives us more grace. That is why Scriptures says,
"God opposes the proud but shows favor to the humble."

When your accomplishments are used to glorify yourself and not God, pride is in control. That's where I was—until God began to deal with me.

When we started pushing for change in the Girl Scouts of the USA with the C.R.Y. organization, I was doing very well with my career. I was managing multiple business units, leading change in local organizations, and had started an Executive MBA program—despite not finishing my undergraduate degree (an absolute movement of God). I was active with my kids, coaching their sports team, helping lead my son's Cub Scout troop, engaged at church, etc. The last thing that we needed in our lives was another time sucker.

But this was important, and Patti really wanted to try and make a difference, so I supported her in any way I could. I helped with informational events, created presentations, brainstormed ways to get the word out, and even agreed to run for the local council's board of directors. That was easy.

However, when Patti began to feel that starting a new group was the only path forward, I became very concerned. We really didn't need this in our busy lives. "I" was concerned about it getting in the way of "my" plans, disrupting "my" life, forcing "me" to adjust. I did not strongly voice my thoughts at this point, realizing how selfish it would sound, but I was not fully supportive of the American Heritage Girls' effort early on. I thought, if it was just for our daughter Katy, I would be okay with this new little group. But God had a different idea.

Slowly, the Lord began to reveal His plan for impacting girls and parents through this "little group." He knew, long before I realized, that American Heritage Girls would influence many for His Kingdom.

One particular morning is forever emblazoned on my mind, when I realized God wanted my submission. I was getting ready for work while Patti shared her dream about how to grow AHG. "We need some PR," she said. "Wouldn't it be great if *Reader's Digest* would write an article about American Heritage Girls?"

AHG was still very young, with only a couple thousand members. My thought was "Yeah, right! Fat chance of that happening."

Imagine my reaction later that morning when Patti called to tell me that *Reader's Digest* had left a message on our answering machine saying they wanted to do an interview. What?

You may think this was coincidence. I prayed about it and came to the definitive conclusion that it was God's voice telling me to get on board. I wondered, *How many other signals have I missed? Why did it take a 2x4 across the head for me to realize what He was doing? What is He asking of me?* This was not the first, nor the last, that it took an abrupt smack for me to wake up. I praise Jesus that He expresses His love with such patience and understanding—He certainly transformed my thinking.

Okay, if the Lord is in this, then AHG is something significant, I thought. I am in. "I" can use my business background to grow it. "I" can use my MBA learnings to help with the structure. "I" can use my speaking skills to get the word out. Well, not so fast.

God was not calling me to use those specific strengths. While our Father absolutely provided education and tools in my business life that applied, some very directly to the business side of AHG, my role was not to lead. No question He had set all the pieces in place for me to earn a business degree at the perfect time. He had guided my career path to put me into leadership roles in business. He provided a path for success. But, God's plan for me in AHG was not in a leadership role —instead, I was to be

> God's plan for me in AHG was not in a leadership role —instead, I was to be a behind the scenes supporter. This was not an easy transition for someone carrying an ego and significant pride.

a behind-the-scenes supporter. This was not an easy transition for someone carrying an ego and significant pride.

I must admit I struggled internally with this direction. I'm a very logical guy and to be honest, it just didn't make sense. I believed I had what it took to make this thing a success. It wasn't until I realized it wasn't what I could do for God, but what He could do through me, that I began to understand.

With time and God's guiding hand keeping me where He wanted me, my place with the organization became clearer. Yes, I could take a leadership role and get things done, but He wanted to use my gifts and talents to empower others to discover theirs. God's work was going to be done, and I needed to fit into His plan, not mine.

Ultimately, I realized the success of the organization was to be a demonstration of God's glory, one that could be magnified through my surrender. More than anything else, He was asking for my obedience. He was asking me to humble myself and give up my pride. It has not always been easy. Frankly, it's still not, but the result of my submission is a sense of joy in my heart that can only come from pleasing Him. He says it best in His Word:

> *But following exactly the way that the Lord, your God, commanded you that you may live and prosper, and may have long life in the land which you are to possess* (Deuteronomy 5:33).

God knew I would struggle with not being in a leadership role. To this day, Patti must still deal with me telling her how to "fix this situation," to "capitalize on that opportunity," or how to do this "piece of marketing better." I am still battling pride.

But God helped me deal with this struggle in a pretty unconventional (but extremely effective) way, when He took away my ability to speak.

No, I didn't lose all speech, but anytime I tried to talk about AHG or the faith journey I had been on, I was moved to tears. This was so foreign to me. I was able to speak in front of large business groups and present complicated material professionally, but if you asked me to talk about girls getting to know their Savior in the beauty of His creation, I became an emotional wreck. Clearly my role was not to be a spokesman for AHG.

I also began to realize that I was grappling with my backseat role, in part because of my traditional view of the role I was called to fulfill as a father, husband, and provider. The Holy Spirit began to quietly open my mind to what family leadership means, and my heart to what He truly envisioned for the marriage relationship. I began to see that marriage was intended to be the true definition of partnership, each partner offering his/her support to the other. Sometimes, this meant I was out front, and at other times, Patti was the "front person." But whether I worked behind the scenes or stood with mic in hand, neither was less important to fulfilling God's will in our lives.

The beauty of how God dealt with me in this season was showing me my involvement in AHG wasn't diminished by my inability to speak about God's movement. It did, however, force me to stay quiet and step back. I had to learn to surrender my need to control in order to become more supportive.

I chuckle now, when I think about how well the Lord knew my stubborn streak and the requirement for a more direct approach (another smack in the head). I'm so thankful that He loved me enough to take my speech, so I could get out of the way and allow Him to do His work with Patti. I have enjoyed the opportunity to watch her grow and thrive as the wonderful leader God crafted her to be.

In most every role I now have, I seem to be behind the scenes. Whether as a husband helping calm Patti before a speech, as a board member (I serve on two nonprofit boards), or even in my business, I'm often the guy in the back. Today, I'm good with it, and, again, God has blessed my obedience. At the risk of appearing prideful, I think I'm effective at serving others. I know I find it fulfilling.

I recently had an AHG volunteer come up to me as I was manning a booth. "Thank you for what you do to support American Heritage Girls and your wife's work. You are making a great impact," she said.

Wow! Where did that come from? I thanked her, and then said a prayer under my breath, praising my Father for His grace and guidance.

I don't want to mislead you. Once I surrendered a leadership role in AHG I still struggled from time to time. As I've mentioned before, I'm stubborn and driven, so pride has a way of sneaking its way back into my life. But I have learned that AHG is God's ministry, not ours. As a result, we must trust that God's got this—His leadership is perfect, and His plans are above our ours.

As I write this, I cannot get one thought out of my head. *Why would you as the reader even care about what I am saying?* But then, I think about what God wants for you.

We all have our struggles, and I am just whining about my journey. My prayer is that this may help someone who wrestles with pride, like I did. Or perhaps, someone with a lack of self-esteem (where a lot of prideful behavior comes from), needs a touch from our Father. God is the Great Healer, and He will heal you if you are obedient to Him.

A pride-lesson the Lord has been teaching me, took me years to understand. I realized I wasn't comfortable with my wife blossoming outside our home. Although this may seem old-fashioned, in talking with other men, I believe it's a common (though rarely discussed) struggle. Patti's success outside of our home had left my sense of manhood somehow threatened. And while I was extremely supportive of Patti and helped her get the organization off the ground, there was another underlying, unnamed fear that she might discover someone else more interesting than me.

When we met in third grade in Cincinnati, the pond was pretty small. But as my wife began traveling the country meeting interesting, and often famous and accomplished new people, I worried. With a much wider world at her disposal, would she still see Pat from Pittsburgh as worthy to love?

I am sure many men suffer with a level of insecurity and must battle the lies of the enemy. That was another part of what God was working out in my life. He seemed to say, "You need to trust in me. Be confident that I have bound you two together and support her, because I have plans." I came to see how a marriage that grows into a true partnership is grounded in stability and trust.

I know many women whose husbands are not confident enough to be supportive and to help their wives fulfill what God has called them to do. It is unfortunate on so many levels. For many men, myself included, letting go of ego is difficult. Ken Blanchard says the EGO is Edging God Out.

When we allow God to manage our ego, we can put self aside and support our wives as God intended. I'm still learning, but it is freeing to serve my wife in the role God has chosen for her as she helps so many young women and volunteers. As Ephesians 5:25 says: *Husbands, love your wives, as Christ loved the church and gave himself up for her.* This is a tall order, and yet it is what God has called all men to do.

I believe the marriage relationship offers a unique support structure, and when we allow God as its centerpiece, it will bring forth great fruit. In order to fulfill God's vision for marriage, spouses must work as a team, solid and strong. Spouses need to actively build a partnership. It's not something that happens by default. We have to make daily choices to willingly serve the other's needs before our own.

Today, Patti and I are stronger together and God has brought us specifically to this place in our relationship. Instead of constricting either one of us, we are both free to be who God desires.

This does not change the fact that we, as men, are called to be the leaders in our homes, regardless of who's making the money or who's got the title at work. We're responsible for the faith of our family. We are accountable for the upbringing of our children. Again, scripture provides us the example of ultimate leadership.

> *"For the husband is the head of the wife even as Christ is the head of the church, his body, and is himself its Savior"* (Ephesians 5:23).

Christ built up the church. Following the biblical plan God has for us as men and women will guide the success of the family.

The Biblical model of the family is part of His redeeming plan. Death can also be a part of that plan.

HAVE YOU CONSIDERED . . .

• *Pride can be debilitating. In your life, have you had instances when pride prevented an opportunity? Have you ever regretted letting your pride control your choices?*

• *Read 1 Timothy 3:2 where it says, "Now the overseer is to be above reproach, faithful to his wife, temperate, self-controlled, respectable, hospitable, able to teach." What does the apostle Paul, who wrote 1 Timothy, say about the virtues of a godly husband? Why are these virtues important?*

• *Have you ever been in a situation where you were unable to release a habit and God forced your hand?*

CHAPTER TWENTY

REDEMPTION

2004

It was a particularly difficult week for my dad. I dreaded walking into his room at Beechwood. I could almost smell death in the air. I tried to control my emotions, holding back my tears, despite knowing these were probably his last days.

During these past weeks, Dad had almost died three times, earning him the nickname Lazarus. During one such episode, we were convinced he died. He had stopped breathing, his face was serene, when suddenly with a jolt, he took a breath. After he came to, he said, "I died, and all I saw were my enemies."

This was disturbing and heartbreaking, because I knew he had no enemies. We could only conclude that because of a serious leg infection and recurring UTIs, his body was full of toxins. This likely affected his mind.

I'll never forget my last visit with him. I quietly stepped into his room and tried not to breathe in deeply. The air was thick with the smell of rotting flesh. I stood there for a minute, watching to make sure my father was breathing. He took shallow breaths, then his inhalations labored, and his chest rattled.

I knew our time was short, and no words could adequately express how much I loved him.

My sister Karen had once asked my dad during a visit what he wanted most out of life. He didn't hesitate and said, "To get up and walk." He never gave up hope. As he lay dying, I knew he would soon be walking on streets of gold. But, oh how I was going to miss him.

Dad died on Friday, March 5, 2004, at the age of 72. He passed, of all things, from decubitus ulcers, bedsores that had burrowed into the bone causing him to become septic. After all the years of suffering and the recent rigorous surgeries to debride his atrophied leg, something preventable ended his life.

Watching him suffer in misery hurt my heart. When he passed, as painful as it was, we knew he was in heaven, pitching ball again.

With his final draw of air, our eighteen years of family Sunday visits to a nursing home were over. The burdens of life with MS were alleviated. And although these years were complete and dad was no longer in pain, we would continue to miss him.

For many weeks afterward, I still checked my phone for a voicemail that said, "It's your dad calling. When you get a chance, give me a ring."

Life with Mom, after Dad's death, changed for me. I was now able to participate in a full relationship with her and not suffer from guilt, as if I were dishonoring my dad. Like the Lord has forgiven me, I found it necessary to forgive my mom. The act of forgiveness can often be difficult, but when fully offered and accepted, it is life giving.

Today, my mom suffers from dementia and resides in a nursing home. She never mentions her nemesis, multiple sclerosis, the disease that defined her for so many years.

In her early stages of dementia, Mom was happy, carefree, and child-like. Nature amazed her. Visits from her children delighted her. And she was the first to hold any new babies in the family. Today, she is confused and determined to return home. I often wonder where she considers home, but one thing she has made clear—she desperately wants to be there. It makes me consider Heaven and God's desire to bring us home after we've completed our purpose on earth.

God does not waste one single chapter of our life's story or the lessons we've learned. Even through some horrible, humbling times, God taught me that all that really mattered was keeping my heart set on Him. Even when I was unsure I could continue, the Lord taught me perhaps the most important lesson of my lifetime. I need Him. Without Him my attempts are in vain.

God has given me a freedom to be responsible only for loving and seeking His face. Understanding who I am and whose I am makes all the difference. This understanding has brought me joy unimaginable. It has allowed me to release to you, the reader, the real Patti Garibay. It's felt scary to reveal the difficult seasons of my life—my struggles and my heartaches. And I am not naive enough to think that some will not judge me and take advantage of my authenticity. But in the end, truth will always win, so it is best to be authentic and true.

The Lord has called me to this message. His opinion is the only one that matters—He is my audience of one. I know how easy it is to fall prey to sin and find strength enough to say, "I messed up." It takes fortitude to admit our mistakes.

My life experiences are what gives me fire in my belly, to be present and focused every day to fight for girls. My prayer is that revealing my own history will ensure young women do not make the same mistakes I've made. I hope they do not fall into the same snares. I pray they seek God early and discover the joy I have today when they are fifteen years old, rather than finding themselves depressed and struggling with a false image of who they are into adulthood.

I want that for others because I care. I love the Lord, so I love His people. Sometimes empathy may make others think you wear rose-colored glasses that lead you into a state of vulnerability. I think leaders need to realize that honesty and authenticity provide the most powerful type of leadership. But you must also be mentally and spiritually strong, because leadership places you in the sights of targeted arrows and accusations.

The more I share openly with girls, the more I talk about fear, because I know what it is like to live smothered by its darkness. When I was young, I was so full of terror, and today, I understand that "storms are the norm."

Life is full of dark clouds, and to think anything differently is setting yourself up for disappointment. That doesn't mean life is bad. What it means is that life is full of lessons. Storms help you understand the lessons. Mountaintop experiences are great, but it is in the scaling of crags and crevices where we learn to lean on God.

In my teens, I worried whether I could really "do life." I feared I might not be able to balance a checkbook or navigate an airport or understand an insurance claim. There are times as an adult I still feel like that scared little child who is so insecure. We can all fall prey to what Satan says about us, even as mature adults. But the earlier we learn whose we really are, the

> The earlier we learn whose we really are, the better our understanding of how God sees us—beautiful, capable, and worthy—and the more prepared we are to light candles that drive away the dark.

better our understanding of how God sees us—beautiful, capable, and worthy—and the more prepared we are to light candles that drive away the dark.

It is important for today's girls to have a framework where they can develop the skills, ability, and confidence to lead well. The only way they can do that is to have the undergirding of a biblical worldview forged through prayer, godly friendships, and faith-based mentors.

I believe American Heritage Girls provides that framework.

The journey as AHG's leader continues and it provides countless lessons for me. But what about you? Has God pricked your heart to do something for Him, leaving you unsure you have what it takes? If so, let me assure you—you do not have what it takes, but God does.

Maybe there's a darkness driving you crazy. If so, are you the one who is supposed to act?

God often places candles before us in the form of frustration because we see something others don't, or if they do, they aren't willing to exercise obedience. He puts fire in us to push us past our fears. He calls us to reach out and ignite the wicks that make the world a better place, helping us discover purpose in spite of life's pain. We make our greatest difference when we dare to believe in a spark before it becomes a flame.

HAVE YOU CONSIDERED . . .

- *Have you, or anyone you have known, ever had a near-death experience?*

- *Have you ever desperately wanted something that you did not receive on earth, but hoped to see in Heaven?*

- *We see in Ephesians 4:32 we are called to forgive, "Be kind and compassionate to one another, forgiving each other, just as in Christ God forgave you." Have you chosen to forgive someone in your life who was not worthy of forgiveness? What fruits came in your life as a result of that act of pardon?*

FAITHFUL

2020

The Lord God Almighty has invited you to sit at the table He has prepared for you now. Not when you're ten pounds lighter, not when your kids are grown, not when you have your graduate degree, but NOW!

My prayer is that my humble story truly inspires you to make a difference. Go and do what generates that fire in your belly, and don't give up. Finish strong.

In those times when the enemy wants to steal your joy and causes you to doubt, remain steadfast. And listen, for God will speak to you—He always has been, and He will remain faithful until the end of time. He loves you just as you are and deems you capable and dearly beloved.

Habakkuk 3:17–19 The Message (MSG)

17-19 Though the cherry trees don't blossom
and the strawberries don't ripen,
Though the apples are worm-eaten
and the wheat fields stunted,
Though the sheep pens are sheepless

and the cattle barns empty,
I'm singing joyful praise to God.
I'm turning cartwheels of joy to my Savior God.
Counting on God's Rule to prevail,
I take heart and gain strength.
I run like a deer.
I feel like I'm king of the mountain!

Just like Habakkuk, the years have taught me the depth and the breadth of God's faithfulness. His desire for each of us is simply obedience. He will equip you to carry out His calling in your life. You have but one requirement.

Just say yes, and don't be afraid to light a candle in a dark place.

ABOUT THE AUTHOR

For more than two decades, Patti Garibay has been at the forefront of countering the culture by leading girls and women to creating lives of integrity. She is the founder and executive director of American Heritage Girls (AHG), a national Christ-centered leadership and character development program. She helps thousands of girls discover their true identity and purpose in Christ through AHG's transformative programming.

Prior to creating AHG, Patti served for twelve years as an active leader and volunteer in Girl Scouts USA (GSUSA). She was highly influential in sharing the gospel with her troop in West Chester, Ohio. In response to major changes in the direction of GSUSA in 1993, the course of Patti's life changed. She heard the voice of God call her to start something new. Patti drew strength from her wealth of leadership opportunities, her love for her country, and her passion for youth development to take a leap of faith in starting AHG in 1995. Today AHG stands strong with over 52,000 members globally. There are AHG Troops in all fifty states and fifteen countries through the Trailblazer Program.

With fearlessness and authenticity, Patti inspires and motivates audiences with her wisdom and experience with raising Godly girls, following God's calling and teaching youth to serve. She is the host of the *Raising Godly Girls* radio minute featured on thousands of radio station across the nation. Through her work with AHG, Patti continues to create innovative ways to break barriers in reaching girls for Christ in the midst of today's culture. Garibay has been featured in hundreds of media outlets including: Axis' Parenting Teen Summit, Axis' Online Homeschool Convention, FamilyLife Radio, *TIME Magazine, The New York Times*, and she was one of the first guests featured on James Dobson's *Family Talk.* Garibay was named a woman of excellence by the West Chester – Liberty Chamber Alliance in 2004, was named a member of the American Family Association's "40 Faithful" in 2017. She has also appeared on *In the Market with Janet Parshall,* Fox News, *Up for Debate with Julie Roys, The Christian Post,* and was nominated and selected as a Woman of Influence through *LEAD Magazine* in 2017.

Patti and her husband, Pat, are blessed with four grown children—three girls and a boy—six grandsons, and three granddaughters. Patti and her four siblings were raised by a disabled father who lived with MS for forty years before his death in 2004. His encouraging attitude of "why curse the darkness when you can light a candle" inspired Patti as she founded the faith-based interdenominational alternative to the Girl Scouts in 1995. She served American Heritage Girls as its first President and Executive Director. She also served as a volunteer Unit Leader for her AHG Troop for nine years.

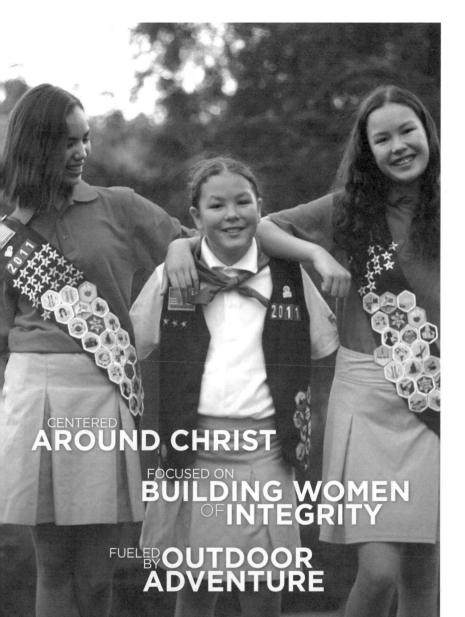

CENTERED
AROUND CHRIST

FOCUSED ON
BUILDING WOMEN
OF**INTEGRITY**

FUELED
BY**OUTDOOR**
ADVENTURE

Learn how you can **JOIN** or **START** a Troop at:
americanheritagegirls.org

AMERICAN
HERITAGE GIRLS®
FAITH | SERVICE | FUN

  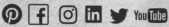